ISBN: 979-8-9851021-3-0

Published by Tommy & Noemi Bradburn. Taos, New Mexico

Printed on acid-free paper.

Tommy Bradburn

First Edition

Table of Contents

1
From a Jack to a Queen

Banfield, Argentina

It was a warm January evening, and Noemi Gonzalez was in a hurry to get home. Dinner with her girlfriends had been fun, but she was ready to relax and to spend some time with her son, Pablo. Work was stressful; word was out that a French corporation planned to buy out the water company where she worked as a district manager. Nobody knew what was going to happen. She didn't know if her job was safe, or if she'd be starting over after 32 years.

Noemi had had enough of starting over. She had been raising Pablo on her own for almost a decade and had finally divorced Pablo's father seven years before. That had caused quite a scandal in the family, and it was almost unheard of in Argentina. Her family was important, and it broke her heart, but she knew it was the right choice. So, she had put aside many of the things she loved, like her friends and her passion for salsa dancing, to focus on the two things that mattered most: her son andher career.

Now, Pablo was 27 and a man and finding his way. They had been discovering a new dimension to their relationship, becoming good friends as well as mother and son. They were travelling and discovering their country together. Most recently, he had taken her skiing at Bariloche, and they had explored new restaurants, enjoyed peacefulstrolls through the snow-covered village, and talked for hours. Noemi was starting to find some time for herself as well, going dancing and going to long dinners with old friends. Now that French company might take it all away.

When Noemi arrived, Pablo wasn't home. It was too bad, but Noemi had another way to blow off steam. She turned on her computer and headed straight for the virtual poker tables at Yahoo.com.

Pablo had been the one to introduce his mother to the wide world of the web. He was fascinated by other countries and cultures and was an expert at making friends online. She saw how much he enjoyed spending time in chat rooms, and one day she realized, "This could be an easy way to sharpen my English skills!" Her beloved father, Roberto, had insisted she learn the language as a child. It had been a great gift, and Noemi knew that gift would fade without practice, so Pablo taught her all about the internet, how to access chat rooms, and where to find new friends. She conversed with people from all over the world.

Of course, that included men. Several of those men had wanted to meet her in person. But Noemi had doubts. She knew that something was missing from her life, and she often wished she could find someone special. She'd been out on a few dates in recent years, but nothing important seemed to be on the horizon. She wasn't going to settle, either. Noemi had suffered when her marriage had failed due to her husband's infidelity, and in losing another relationship to alcohol abuse. She wasn't sold on the idea of another long-term mess. So, she resisted those men's invitations to meet and concentrated on practicing her English conversation skills.

Then one night, bored with the same old conversations, she decided to try something new. Yahoo had ongoing poker games as well as chat rooms. She liked to play cards. Why not give it a try? It turned out to be a life-changing decision.

On this particular night, Noemi was cleaning up at Texas Hold 'Em. She was on a winning streak that was starting to irritate the other players. But she kept taking their chips. Then, suddenly, an instant message popped up. It read:

> You are a poker machine. You are the Poker Queen!

The screen name was "Miller Chime." Not one of the other players. Who could that be?

Denton, Texas, USA

Tom Bradburn slowed down on the highway to let an 18-wheeler pass. Today, like every day for the past 3 years, he was fighting Dallas traffic to get home. Mentally, he tried to let go of the stresses of the day. He had recently cut back his workload from supervising 16 Sonic Drive-In restaurants to 5, but it was still tough to balance that with being a single parent. This traffic wasn't helping. His teenage son, Eric, would be waiting at home, and Tom turned his thoughts to what he'd cook for dinner. He decided on pork chops and French fries, Eric's favorite.

At last, he pulled into his parking spot at the apartment complex. He could see Eric standing outside, waiting for him. Walking to the door,he shivered a little in the cool January breeze. Then they threw their arms around each other, as usual, and walked inside.

Unfortunately, Tom's worries didn't stop when he entered the small apartment. Though they were close, he and Eric had been struggling recently. At 17, his son had decided he didn't like going to school. And like any unsupervised teen would be tempted to do, he had been skipping a lot lately. Tom's work didn't leave time for the close parentalattention Eric needed. They both hated these conversations, but Tom knew they'd have to discuss it this evening.

From the kitchen, he called, "How was school today?"

In front of the TV, Eric called back. "Great!"

Tom didn't buy it. "Really?"

"Well, it was ok." Eric's tone was laid back. Too laid back.

"Have any homework?"

"I did it at school."

Tom couldn't help sounding disbelieving. "Eric. Did you really?"

"Of course. Don't you believe me?"

Quickly, Tom added, "It doesn't matter whether I believe you or not. What matters is your life and what you're doing with it."

"Dad, don't start, ok?"

In the silence, the pan began to sizzle. He heard Eric's voice again, "What's for dinner?"

"Pork chops."

"All right!" Suddenly, life was good again.

After dinner, Tom washed the dishes while Eric dried, just like they had done every night since his son was 10. He knew that when they were done, Eric would retreat to his favorite video game, "The Legend of Zelda." He might as well plan to spend the evening on the computer he'd recently bought. Tom frowned as he pictured Eric on the living room floor, absorbed in Zelda, and himself in front of the screen in the bedroom. That seemed to be their world for the last few weeks. He didn't like that they no longer seemed to talk much, but Tom toldhimself, "At least we're together."

One thing Tom did like about his nights in front of the computer, it had reawakened one of his earliest passions: silver coins. In the early 1960s, Tom had worked as a carhop for a quaint little drive-in called Carroll's. Back then, everyone paid in silver coins. Tom loved them; they were beautiful. And he looked back with fondness on that job. As a young man, he had bigger aspirations than being a carhop. Of course, but he had enjoyed running the trays of orders out to waiting cars. And thatwas where he had seen his first Sonic, built right across the street from Carroll's in 1965. Tom had been hired by Sonic soon after it opened, and except for two years in the Marine Corps, Sonic would be Tom's professional home for over 37 years.

He was growing tired of the fast-food business, after so many years of service, and he was worried about his son, so his computer was awelcome distraction. Tom learned how to research and buy silver coins using the Internet. For the past six months, he had been buying cases of beautiful, untouched, uncirculated Silver Eagle dollars. Tonight, he had nine cases of 500 coins, each stacked on the floor next to his desk. He looked at the boxes, feeling fortunate that the coins inside were all his.

But tonight, he decided to try something different. He glanced at his Yahoo page. His eye caught the words "Yahoo Poker." Tom clicked the link.

That click opened an entirely new world, Tom created an account so he could access the virtual tables, and found one called "Hound Dog" that sounded good. An oval tabletop filled his screen. Nine chairssurrounded it, each with a little nametag in front of it on the table, with screen names on each one. In each chair sat a little cartoon character, representing a player somewhere in the real world. Tom could also see stacks of chips in front of each player, and each place showed two cards turned face down. In the center of the table sat five cards turned face up.Tom realized that he was watching Texas Hold 'Em. The table was full so that he couldn't join in, but that was ok. He was watching andlearning.

"The Internet is amazing!" he thought. It was pretty cool the way everyone could bet and fold and win and take their winnings. Theplayers could type messages to one another, like "Good hand" or "You dirty dog."

After a few minutes, he noted that one player, a cartoon girl with a blonde ponytail, seemed to be taking everyone's chips. "Noemigonz" was on a winning streak. The other players were getting annoyed, which Tom found comical. On a whim, he clicked her name to send an instant message:

You are a poker machine. You are the Poker Queen!

The reply came back:

Thank you… What is Miller Chime?

And just like that, the life-changing conversation began.

> *Tom: Have you ever heard of "Miller Time?"*
> *Noemi: No*
> *Tom: Miller is a beer in the U.S. Their advertisement says, "It's Miller Time"…I tried to make my Yahoo name Miller Time but it was taken. So, I came up withMiller Chime.*
> *Noemi: Oh, ok.*
> *Tom: My name is Tom, what is yours?*
> *Noemi: Noemi…I'm pleased to meet you, Tom.*
> *Tom: I'm glad to meet you, Noemi.*
> *Tom: How long have you been playing?*
> *Noemi: About 15 minutes.*
> *Tom: No, I mean, how many years have you been playing Texas Hold 'em?*
> *Noemi: Ha. Sorry…2 years.*
> *It's a fun game; you should play.*
> *Tom: I'd rather talk to you right now.*
> *Noemi: Thank you, would you like to go to a private room?*

Tom still didn't know a lot about the Internet, but he had heard of cybersex. He wondered, "Does this mean we're about to have sex right here online?" He told Noemi that he didn't understand, and she explained that a private room was a safe place to chat where no one could read what they said. Ok, so maybe not sex. Tom typed in,

Oh, ok…But I don't know how to do that.

Noemi promised that she'd take care of it and be right back. Then a box popped up on Tom's screen that read:

> *Someone wants to chat with you. Click here to chat with them.*

Tom clicked, and another box popped up.

> *Noemi: Hello.*
> *Tom: Hello, poker Queen.*
> *Noemi: "Ha-ha...I like to play; you should try it.*
> *Tom: I will someday, but right now, I am happy that Yahoo Poker allowed me to meet you.*
> *Noemi: Yes, I am also glad for that.*
> *Tell me about you. Where do you live? Do you have children?"*
> *Tom: I live in Denton, Texas, and I have 2 sons; Eric and Jeff. How about you?*
> *Noemi: Very nice names, Eric and Jeff.*
> *I live in Buenos Aires, Argentina, and I have one son. His name is Pablo.*
> *Tom: Wow...we are very far from one another.*
> *This is the first time I have ever done anything like this. How did you know how to open a private chat?*
> *Noemi: My son taught me.*

Tom sat back in his chair, clasped his hands behind his head, and thought, "Wow." This was his first experience with Internet chat, and his excitement ran wild.

> *Noemi: You are not married, are you?*
> *Tom: No. Are you?*
> *Noemi: Oh, no, I am not married.*

Tom suddenly remembered something else he'd read about the Internet.

> *Tom: I am a man. I suppose you are a woman, huh?*
> *Noemi: Oh, yes. I am a woman. ... This is difficult. Isn't it?*
> *Tom: Oh well, this is about as good as chat gets, I suppose. If you give me your email address, I will send you an email and tell you about me.*
> *Noemi: Okay. It is* <u>*noemigonz@cbs.com*</u>*, and what is your address?*
> *Tom:* <u>*tcb3@airmail.net*</u>
> *Noemi: Okay, thanks.*
> *Tom: I will go and send you an email now. Okay?*
> *Noemi: Okay, that will be great.*
> *Tom: Bye for now.*
> *Noemi: Bye...Pleased to meet you.*

After signing off, Noemi went to the refrigerator for some water, she thought about this Tom guy. "Is he a real person?" she wondered. "Will he send me an e-mail?" She stared out the window for a few moments, thinking about the evening. Then she smiled and headed for bed.

Meanwhile, Tom typed, full of a new kind of excitement. He told this Noemi woman all about his life, his job, his family, and his past. He searched to learn about her. Then, seeing it was late, he turned off the computer and called Eric to get ready for bed.

"Who were you writing to on the computer?" his son asked.

"Just some girl from Argentina."

"Argentina?! What can you do with a woman in Argentina?"

Tom chuckled, "Just talking, Son, just talking."

In bed, he lay awake for a long time, wondering about this Argentina lady. Who was she? What kind of life did she have? At last, his brainfull of questions, Tom drifted off to sleep.

2

A Picture's Worth a Thousand Words

Banfield, Argentina

Noemi woke up, wondering how soon it would be before she got an e- mail from Mr. Miller Chime. Not long at all—it was waiting in herinbox when she turned on her computer. "There it is!" she thought, excitedly clicking. As she read, a line often made her laugh out loud. Then the next line would make her stop and think. Her face flickered from smiles to seriousness, and when she finished, at last, she paused to consider this Tom guy. Then she got busy replying with an e-mail of her own.

Noemi enjoyed the thrill of writing a stranger in the U.S., but she was cautious, too. As she described her son, her job, past relationships, her friends and family, she chose her words carefully. Then, when she finished, she read the letter several times. At last, she clicked send.

Denton, Texas, USA

The day was long, and traffic was awful again, but his anticipation buoyed Tom. As soon as he got in the door, he gave Eric a distracted hello and headed straight to his computer. There was an e-mail from Noemi. A long one. The Argentina lady had almost written a book, telling Tom all about her life. In the end, she had accepted his invitation to chat at 7 p.m., so Tom hurried to the Yahoo chat room. There shewas, waiting.

Noemi: Hello, Tom.
Tom: Hi Noemi, how was your day?
Noemi: Today was a fine day for me, but it was very long waiting to chat with you.
Tom: Yep. I know the feeling. I've been excited to chat with you all day.
I received your email today, very nice.
Noemi: It was your email that gave me much to speak. So, both of your sons are of the same mother?
Tom: No, different wives.
Noemi: So, you have been married 2 times?
Tom: No, I've been married 4 times.

...

Noemi: Wow.
Tom: Yes, I know.
Noemi: How can anyone be married 4 times?
Tom: I'm not sure, but I was."
I would not change anything because everything I have done has made me the man that I am today.
Noemi: Yes, but why have you been married 4 times?

"Well, that's the end of that," thought Tom. He knew it was hard for most people to understand how a person could have that many failed relationships. It was even harder to talk about because life was too complicated for simple explanations.

There had been no lack of love between Tom and his first wife, his high school sweetheart. Unfortunately, 20 days after their wedding, the U.S. Marine Corps shipped him off to Vietnam for a 13-month tour. For the first two months, he was a machine gunner. It was miserable. The men were all soaking wet every day. The mosquitos were awful, the food sucked, and the nightly firefights were worse. Every day, he lost friends.

Then Tom received a call to report to the company office. He boarded the chopper that would deliver him there, wondering what they could want with him. The First Sergeant called Tom into the office, and he stood silent while the officer looked over his records. Then the sergeant said, "I see you took a typing test in boot camp. How would you like to leave the bush and work in the office?"

Tom knew he had only typed about 12 words a minute and had made about 1,000 mistakes, but he replied, "I'd love that!" That little typing test may have saved Tom's life. He became the unit diary clerk for Lima Company. While he was not totally out of danger, he was away from the trials and tribulations of the bush. Each day, his duties included taking inventory of wounded or killed Marines, which was a heartbreaking task. He counted the days until he could return home.

When he reached 52 days before the end of his tour, Tom got a pack of playing cards. Each day he mailed a card to his wife. The day he mailed the last card, he boarded a plane for home.

The journey back to his wife in Denton, TX, included a stop in San Diego, CA. As he and the other troops deplaned, they faced an angry crowd of civilians. People cussed and screamed "Baby killers" or threw cups full of soda. The men got away as quickly as they could. In the restroom, cleaning themselves off, Tom and the others wondered aloud what country they were in. What the heck was going on? How was it possible that they had felt more at home in Vietnam than they did intheir own country? Sad, angry, and confused, the men walked out to the ticket counters to buy the flights that would take them to their destinations.

In Dallas, at last, he fell into his wife's arms. His mom, stepfather, brother, and sisters were there to welcome him with tears, hugs, laughter, and smiles. He felt safe and welcome at last. But within a few months, new problems began.

Newly stationed in California, Tom woke in the middle of the night and thought he had a heart attack. His wife rushed him to the base hospital. There, the doctors explained that his experience was an anxiety attack. They gave him some medication to help him relax, and they returned home. For the next six months, things seemed fine. He finished his service in the Marines, and the couple returned to Denton. Tom went back to the Sonic Drive-In and got an offer as a job of assistant manager. It seemed they were settling into a new life...then it happened again, another anxiety attack. This one lasted most of a day. He called the VA, and they made him an appointment.

When Tom arrived, he realized the doctor was a psychiatrist. Thispuzzled him, but he told the doctor his problem. Then they both satsilent for an hour. It was as if each was waiting for the other to speak, but neither did. Once the physiatrist finished the hour, he scheduledTom for another appointment. This went on for five sessions before Tom decided he was better off just focusing on his work.

And Tom was good at his job. First, he was offered a promotion by his current employer. Then, he got an opportunity to help open a brand-new Sonic Drive-In, with a 10% ownership share. He jumped at the chance. He and his wife soon moved to Blytheville, AR. For the next two years, Tom threw himself into the management of this new location. It became the highest profit Sonic Drive-In in America. And during that time, she gave birth to their son.

But Tom could not easily balance the demands of his job, the pace of his lifestyle, a new wife, and the responsibility of a new child all at the same time. It also did not help those strange bouts of anxiety, nightmares, or anger continued to happen. He could not understandquite how it came about, because he still loved her deeply, but their marriage ended in divorce.

Things only got more complex for Tom after that. He foundprofessional freedom and success through opening new Sonic locations in partnership with the landlord from the Blytheville site. He continued to struggle with post-traumatic anxiety attacks and learned to overcome them alone. Over the years, he married and divorced three more times.

Then, after the end of his third marriage, Eric's mother decided she could not care for their son and gave Tom full custody. After several years of moving from place to place and struggling to balance work with child-raising, Tom finally decided he needed to simplify his life. He sold his interest in the Sonic Drive-Ins he owned and co-owned, and took a supervisor job for a group of 16 locations, and settled permanently in Denton.

But how do you say all that to a woman you have just met online? Instead, Tom wrote:

> *Tom: Well, American women are funny creatures. All but one of them was after money.*
> *Noemi: "Okay. Now I understand…"*
> *Noemi: "Tell me about your boys."*
> *Tom: Jeff is my oldest son. He is 26. He is a very smart young man and has a great job. He started at the University of Texas but just graduated from the University of North Texas with a degree in Business Administration.*
> *Noemi: You must be very proud.*
> *Tom: Eric is my youngest. He is 17. He is going through a bad time, but he is very smart, and he will get back on track. I love them both very much.*
> *Noemi: I am so happy to hear that.*
> *I also love my son. He is very smart and is a good boy.*
> *Noemi: I am anxious to know what you look like. Can you send a photo?*
> *Tom: I will try, but I have never sent photos before. Maybe you can send me a photo of you as well?*

> *Noemi: Yes. I don't know how either, but my son will do it for me.*
> *Mr. Tom, it is getting very late here so I should go to bed now.*
> *Tom: I'm sorry. I know that it is 3 hours later there. You sleep like a queen, and I will chat with you tomorrow. Bye for now.*
> *Noemi: bye.*

Sitting back in her chair, Noemi tried to process what she had just learned — married four times? Was that going to be an issue? She hoped not. Though she had some concerns, she was more curious than anything else. What did this mystery man look like?

Tom decided to take the next morning off and get the photo done. This seemed easy enough. But it turned out to be a lot more complicated than he planned. First, it took a while to decide what to wear. Then he drove to a nearby park with a pond and trees. He set his camera on the branch of a tree, set the timer for 15 seconds, and then he ran to pose in front of the lens. He went back to the camera only to discover that they had chopped his whole head off in the shot. How to fix that? In the end, he built a small tripod from tree bark to stabilize the camera and got his perfect shot.

Next was a stop at the computer store. He explained to the guy at the counter that he was "Technology deprived," and asked for help transferring the photo and e-mailing it. Tom watched in amazement as the clerk attached the camera to the computer using a cable, and then pushing a single button. Bing bang bong. The photo was now on hishard drive. Then the clerk asked for Noemi's address, clicked a few keys, and whoosh away went the photo to Argentina. Tom went home happy as a lark, changed his clothes, and went to work.

Noemi rushed straight to her computer when she got home that evening. An e-mail from Tom waited in her inbox. But when she opened the message—nothing! No photo! She jumped up and rushed into the next room, grabbed her son Pablo by the hand, and dragged him back to the computer with her. Her son grinned as he clicked a few keys, and bing bang bong, there was Tom's image.

The photo showed a nice-looking man in a dark blue flannel shirt, unbuttoned, with a white t-shirt underneath. A New York Yankees ball cap covered his hair. He stared at the camera with a serious expression

"Good-looking man," Pablo commented.

"Oh Pablo, he's beautiful!" Noemi sighed. She stared, entranced, and then remembered, "I promised I would send him a photo, too! You haveto help me send it."

"No problem." Pablo found a recent picture of the two of them, standing together in the kitchen, scanned it, and sent it off to Tom. Then he turned to his mother. She was still staring at Tom's photo, smiling to herself. Quietly, he left the room.

Tom was also in a hurry to get home from work. This was the days of dial-up, and the wait for his e-mail to load seemed longer than ever. He had enough time to clean up and change clothes before his messages were ready. And there was one from Noemi. But when he opened it— nothing! No photo!

Tom switched over to Yahoo Messenger, and there Noemi was waiting. She didn't even wait for him to say hello before she started typing.

> *Noemi: Oh, Baby, you are beautiful.*
> *Tom: Well, thank you. I guess you got the photo.*
> *Noemi: Yes, and I have studied it very well.*
> *Tom: Ha-ha. You are very funny.*
> *Noemi: I did not tell you a joke; you are beautiful.*
> *Did you receive my photo?*
> *Tom: No.*

Noemi knew just what to do. She ran and got her son. Once again, it was Pablo to the rescue. Just as he had done for his mother, Pablo explained to Tom how to look for a little paper clip icon in the top right of the e-mail window and click on it. Tom did as he said exactly.

With the sluggish connection, the image opened very slowly. At last, he could see it. There she was, standing next to a handsome young man. He wasn't a fan of her black leather pants, but her face and her eyes were so beautiful that they hooked Tom.

And of course, Yahoo Messenger picked that moment to crash. Couldn't anything be easy today? Tom tried reconnecting. Nothing. He triedagain and again, desperate as a man could be. Finally, he turned off the computer, waited for five endless minutes, and turned it on again. As quickly as possible, he went back to Yahoo.

> Tom: Hello.
>
> ...
>
> Noemi: Hello.
> Tom: Wow, I thought you were gone.

Noemi: No, no. I thought you looked at my photo and decided that you were not interested.
Tom: Oh, not at all. I lost my connection and could not reconnect.
Noemi: I'm sorry you were disconnected, but happy I did not lose you.
Tom: You will never lose me.
Noemi: I was very sad, and Pablo was trying to cheer me up, but now I am very happy.
Tom: You have the most beautiful eyes. I love them, and yes, you are the Queen.
Noemi: Thank you, baby, but now I am embarrassed.
Tom: You have no reason to be embarrassed. Very nice photo. Beautiful woman.
One question? Who is the man in the photo with you?
Noemi: That is Pablo. I told him not to send that photo.
Tom: Oh, okay. I'm glad you sent that photo so I could also see your son.
Noemi: He's a very good boy.
Tom: I can see that.
Noemi: Baby, I am so excited, but it is very late, and I need to go to bed. I will sleep with your photo in my brain tonight.
Tom: I love that you are calling me Baby. I will talk with you tomorrow at 7 pm. Sleep well.
Tom: Bye for now.
Noemi: Good night, Baby.

Noemi looked at Tom's photo and how he seemed to be a healthy and strong man. She liked how he spoke to her. She hoped he wasn't too good to be true. Pablo helped her print the image, and the next day, she took it to work. She showed it to her friends at lunch, her face glowing with excitement.

In his chair in front of the computer, Tom thought about this woman calling him "Baby." It felt a little strange, but he liked it. He stared at her photo, thinking that she looked like a happy person. He hoped she wasn't too good to be true.

3
Getting to Know You

For the next five months, Tom and Noemi chatted every night and sent constant emails back and forth. At the end of each day, in his car, Tom would think, "I can't wait to get home and chat with her." The conversations were relaxed, fun, and sometimes funny. As he typed, he could always picture her smiling face.

As the weeks and months passed, they became more comfortable sharing their concerns and frustrations. Noemi described the changes in her company and how anxious she had been about her job security. She shared her relief when the new French owners saw the contribution she made and came to value her.

Tom spoke about the stresses of his job, the anxieties of dealing with several managers at his Sonic locations, and the terrors of Dallas's consistent traffic. He also admitted that he and Eric were having a very difficult time. Noemi always understood.

Tom: He is in a bad place. The boys that are his friends smoke marijuana and cigarettes. A few weeks ago, we had a terrible fight, and I threw him out of the house. I haven't seen him since.

Noemi: I'm sorry about Eric. My son also tried marijuana, but I stopped it right away. He and his friends would get together and smoke it. When I found out, I called a meeting with all of the boy's parents and we put an end to it.

At one point, the two exchanged phone numbers. One morning, at 5:30, Tom's phone rang. "Who the heck would call so early?" he thought. He picked up, and a strange female voice on the other end of the line said, "Hello Baby."

"Is this Noemi?"

"Yes, it is me."

The first few minutes of the call were difficult. Noemi was out of practice with spoken English conversation, and her sentences were a bit broken. Tom sometimes had to translate into his brain. And she struggled to understand Tom. Finally, she asked him to slow down.

"Sorry," Tom laughed, "I guess I am a fast talker."

"It's ok, Baby. I wanted to hear how your voice sounds."

"And how does it sound?"

"Now that you are speaking slowly, your voice sounds great."

"Well, so does yours."

Gradually, the conversation became more relaxed. But Noemi eventually sighed, "I'm sorry, but I have to go to work now. I hope I didnot interrupt your sleep too much."

Tom protested, "No, I am very glad you called. I will chat with you again tonight at 7 pm."

"Okay. Nice to finally hear your voice."

"Nice to hear your voice as well. Bye for now." Tom hung up the phone, thinking how stupid he must have sounded trying to wake up enough to converse. "I hope she doesn't think I'm a clown," he thought. He wondered if he should go back to bed or stay up. He was probably too keyed up to go back to sleep, so he put the coffee on and thought of

Noemi. What a surprise it was to hear her voice, South American and sexy, even if it took a few minutes to understand her words.

Noemi hung up her phone, pleased at how well the conversation had gone. She realized she had probably woken Tom too early, but she was glad that his voice matched his photo. "But that accent will be something to deal with," she thought.

The day passed slowly for both of them as they relived the morning's conversation and anticipated that night's chat. Noemi couldn't wait to hear Tom's feelings about their call. She could tell she was falling in love with this wonderful Texas man. "We have shared all of our thoughts during the past several months," she considered, "All exceptfor one thing... Sex!" She decided it was time to bring up that subject tonight.

Tom was busy examining his own emotions too. He spent all day thinking about how sweet Noemi was and how bold she had been tocall. He was experiencing feelings he had not had for many years now. The experience was exciting, but confusing, too. Mentally, they had spent so much time together over the past several months. They had chatted about everything that two people could possibly discuss. He'd seen her picture, and now he'd heard her voice. But was that enough?He wondered, "How could I possibly feel this way about a woman that Ihave never met?" Then he shook his head and told himself, "Calm down, you idiot. She lives in Argentina, and I live in Texas. What could come of this?" Nevertheless, he couldn't wait to talk to her at night.

> Tom: Hello Noemi, how was your day?
> Noemi: Hello Baby, my day was wonderful after hearing your voice this morning.
> Tom: Yes, I was very anxious to get home tonight to chat with you.
> Noemi: Really? What are you thinking?

Tom: "I was thinking of how thankful I am that you called.
Noemi: You mean that my voice did not scare you away?
Tom: Are you kidding? Today I thought that we have chatted about all of our feelings, we have seen each other's photos and now we have heard each other's voices. We have done it all.
Noemi: Well, not all.
Tom: What do you mean?
Noemi: We haven't talked about sex.
Tom: I love sex. Is that what you mean?
Noemi: That is what I mean.
Tom: Well, what do you want to know?
Noemi: What do you like about sex?
Tom: I like everything about sex.
Noemi: I'm glad to hear that because I think we might be very good together.

...

Tom: Are you okay?
Noemi: "Oh, I am better than okay, I am reaching heaven."
Tom: Should I help you to get there?

A short while later, Tom and Noemi sat back in their respective chairs, breathless. They had just had heavenly computer sextogether.

Noemi: That was great, Baby. I cannot wait to hold you and kiss you.

Tom: Well, I don't know what to say about that. I cannot leave my job right now; it is the beginning of the high season.

Noemi: I have my vacation coming up next month. I can come to see you. I want to know you better.

Tom: Wow! Do you really want to come here?

Noemi: Yes, of course.

Tom: I would be happy to pay for your trip.

Noemi: Don't worry, Pablo's' father works for an airline, and I can get free tickets.

Tom: Wow! That is great, just let me know when.

Noemi: Yes, I will work on that.
Baby, you have made me so relaxed, and it is getting late. We probably need to go to bed now.

Tom: Yes. Thank you for this night. I am also relaxed. Sleep well.

Noemi: I feel great right now, and I know that I will dream of you tonight. I would love to feel you next to me right now.

Tom: You are a very exciting woman...I will also dream of us tonight. Sleep well.

Noemi: It's very hard to say goodbye, but we should. Good night, Baby.

Noemi and Tom fell asleep quickly, but the next morning, both woke with minds running wild. Tom couldn't believe the night had actually happened, or the rush of excitement as a woman more than 5,000 miles away had given him sex while on the computer. Noemi was warm, thinking how good Tom had made her feel, and how much she loved that he had not been bothered a bit by her words and actions. "I cannot wait to meet him," she thought, "I think he may be perfect for me."

She spent the next few days planning her trip. She spoke to Pablo's father, and he agreed to help her with tickets to Dallas (though shecalled it a "business trip" and didn't mention the man she was going to meet). She searched all the flights, and then made her reservation for May 16th, full of hope that everything would come together just as she had dreamed.

Things didn't go as smoothly when she told her friends over lunch. The laughter at the table stopped when she mentioned her plans, and the arguments began. She was loco; she needed to be careful. This man could be dangerous. Noemi just smiled and said, "We will see."

Thankfully, Noemi knew that her son would understand. A couple of years earlier, Pablo had spent several months chatting online with one young lady from Canada. Eventually, he had told his mother that he planned to go there and visit her. Noemi had found it hard to understand why Pablo wasted his time on the computer, talking to a girl far away. She was nervous about her baby travelling the world alone, but he was a man now, not a boy. He would be fine. She kept her mouth closed and let him go. When he returned a month later, he told Noemi that the trip had shown him this young lady would not be his connection for life, but the experience had been valuable. So, before her 7 p.m. Yahoo date that evening, Noemi had a little chat with Pablo about her plans. He immediately realized that his mother was in the same spot he'd been in two years ago, making the same decision. He was happy and excited for her. So, Noemi was able to meet Tom with a light heart.

Noemi: Hello, Baby.
Tom: Hello, how was your day?
Noemi: I had the best day that I have had in a
while.Tom: Oh, really? Tell me about it.
Noemi: I bought a ticket to Dallas today. Just think,
in two weeks, on May 16th, we will finally meet, and
I amso excited.
Tom: Wow. I didn't expect this to happen so quickly.
Noemi: Are you sad that it is happening so quickly?
Tom: Absolutely not. I am extremely happy, just
surprised.
Noemi: Tell me, what type of house do you have?
Tom: Well, it is actually an apartment, and I would
describe it as humble. It is small, and it is old, but it
has everything that I need. The post office is close by,
my mailbox is next to my front door, and there are a
washing machine and dryer next door to my
apartment.I like it here.
Noemi: I will see it very soon, but even more
important,I will see you very soon.
Tom: Yep, it's getting exciting now.
Let's see; May 16th is on Sunday. That is good because
Idon't work on that day, then I will plan some things
forus to do while you are here.
Noemi: Well, Baby, it's late, and we need to sleep.
Tom: Yes...You sleep well. Only 2 more weeks and I
willbe able to hold you in my arms and kiss your lips.
Noemi: Don't say those
things.Tom: Why not?
Noemi: Because I will be like a child at Christmas
Tom: Ha-ha. Funny.

After they signed off, Tom looked around his apartment. He realized he had to get off his butt and clean the place up. It looked like a single guy lived there, and not in a good way.

For the next two weeks, Tom and Noemi chatted every night. They were like children. They laughed, they cried but most of all, they had fun and enjoyed every moment.

Noemi: Hello, baby, how are you today?

Tom: I am excited about your trip in only 2 days...hard to believe.

Noemi: Yes, but I have a lot to do before then. It's difficult for a woman to pack for 2 weeks.

Tom: Yep, it's great to be a man.

Noemi: Let me ask you a question?

Tom: Okay.

Noemi: If things worked out for us, where would you like to live? I've been studying North Carolina, and it looks very nice. It is on the beach and not far from the mountains. What do you think?

Tom: You are very confident that things will work out for us.

Noemi: Well, we have talked for 5 months, and I feel very good about you. We will see what happens. I was only thinking.

Tom: So, you are willing to live in the U.S.?

Noemi: Of course, I would love to live in the U.S. I could still visit Argentina.

> Tom: Of course you can.
> North Carolina sounds good, but I would like isolation more. Maybe in the mountains in Montana.
> Noemi: I like mountains, too. I will search for Montana, and we will see.
> Tom: Sounds great, we will see.

Each day, Tom thought about Noemi as he worked his stores. He considered that for almost 5 months, they had become as close as two people can be even though they had never met one another. The thought about Montana, and the more he thought about it, the more he liked the idea. On the day before her arrival, he told an employee at one of the restaurants about her visit. The woman exclaimed, "Argentina? How do you know a woman from Argentina?"

Tom laughed, "Just lucky, I guess." But he was nervous, too. He hoped there would be no language problems, and that communication would be easy. Most of all, he hoped they both just fell into each other's arms and felt comfortable.

Noemi was nervous, too, as she rushed through the preparations. She could barely concentrate on packing as she dreamed of that crazy man in Texas. Would they be a match? If everyone talked as fast as Tom, would she be able to understand anyone?

Finally, they met for their last 7 p.m. chat before her flight in the morning.

Noemi: Hello, Baby.

Tom: Hello, how was your day?

Noemi: Very busy, I tried to pack, but I could not get you off my mind, so I hope that I packed everything.

Tom: Ha-ha. If you forget something, we will buy it here. Don't worry. Just remember to bring yourself, and we will have a happy time.

Noemi: Ha-ha. Yes, I was thinking about the trip, and I hope that you like what you see.

Tom: You funny lady, I have seen your photo and talked with you on the phone and chatted with you for 5 months now, and I can tell you that I will love what I see.

Noemi: Thank you. I needed to hear that I feel better now.

Noemi: Baby, I have to get up very early tomorrow for the trip. I need to leave my apartment at 4 a.m., so I need to try and get some sleep.

Tom: Wow. 4 a.m. That is very early. I hope you can get some good sleep tonight.

Noemi: If I don't, I will have plenty of time to sleep on the plane.

Tom: I hate sleeping on a plane.

Noemi: I do too, but I need to rest for you for us.

Tom: Okay. Go and sleep well, and I will see you tomorrow.

Noemi: I can't believe that I will finally see you.

Tom: Bye for now and have a good trip tomorrow.

Noemi: Bye, Baby. I can't wait to see you. You sleep well, also.

4
Hello Texas

Buenos Aires, Argentina

Noemi and Pablo sat at the airport with coffee and croissants. She had barely slept a wink the night before, and now she was almost too excitedto speak. Pablo laughed at her. "Relax, Mom. I saw his photo, and he seems like a good man, just have a good time; everything will be ok.

"I know, but you know how I am. I have to worry about everything."

"No one knows better than I do."

At last, it was time to board the plane. Pablo left Noemi at the security check-in and waved as she walked out of sight. Then she was gone on her new adventure.

Denton, Texas, USA

Tom was a mess. An Argentina woman was coming to see him. "This is the craziest thing that has ever happened to me," he thought. He spent the morning visiting three of his restaurants, hardly concentrating on what he was doing.

Then he turned the car toward the DFW airport, growing more nervous every mile. "Wow," he kept repeating to himself, "just wow."

DFW Airport

Tom searched the arrivals board for Noemi's gate. It was a long walk, but he was 30 minutes early. Finally, the plane arrived. Tom stood to watch as the passengers emerged. Five people, then 20, then 100, 200, then the people stopped. No Noemi. He didn't understand. Tom went to the gate agent, who checked the passenger list. There was no Noemi Gonzalez on the flight.

Now Tom felt stupid. "What on earth could I possibly be thinking that a woman from Argentina would come to see me?" He sat down as he tried to think this mess through. He decided to check another AmericanAirlines gate to make sure he hadn't gotten the flight number wrong,and then another and then another. No Noemi. After an hour of walking around and not finding Noemi, Tom decided that he was an idiot, and heleft the airport.

Driving home, Tom made a decision. Even without that Noemi woman, he was going to Montana. And why not in a new car? When he arrived in Denton, he went to see a friend who worked at a car dealership. Tom picked out a four-wheel-drive Ranger pickup, and together, they went inside to close the deal. Just as he was signing the papers, he got a page. It was a number he didn't recognize. This was in the days before everyone had a cell phone, so Tom paid for the car and headed home to call.

Noemi stepped off the plane in Dallas at last. She was exhausted. She had missed 2 flights in Miami and was more than 2 hours late. She looked around the gate area, but she could not see Tom. There was a crowd of people meeting friends and family, so she waited, anxiously looking back and forth. Eventually, the gate cleared — no Tom. Noemi was heartbroken. She thought, "How stupid I am to think that a man from Texas wanted to meet a woman from Argentina."

She didn't know what to do. She was in a strange airport in a strange state in a strange country. Should she get a hotel room to rest, thenfigure out a plan tomorrow? She got so nervous she began to forget her English. She went to the counter and asked for someone who spoke Spanish, and a gate agent came forward. Noemi explained her situation and asked the agent to search the phone book to see if Tom Bradburn existed. Noemi held her breath while the woman looked, the agentfound the number, reads the address, and yes, it was the correct one. The agent called the number, but no one answered. Noemi's eyes filled with tears. The agent gently asked, "Do you have another way to contact him? Another number?" Noemi suddenly remembered that Tom had a pager. She gave the number to the agent, who sent a page from the phone at the gate.

At home, Tom dialed the unfamiliar number. A strange voice said, "Wait a moment, please." Then he heard Noemi's familiar accent, "Oh Baby, what happened? I have been at the airport searching for you."

"I was there, and you were not on the flight."

"Oh, Baby, I flew standby, and I missed two planes and arrived here late."

"Okay, I will be there in about 45 minutes, please wait at the baggage claim."

"I will wait, but hurry, please."

Tom promised, "I will. I'll be there as quickly as I can.

At the baggage claim, Tom searched. Once again, he could not see Noemi. Then, from a distance, he saw a lone woman walking toward him, smiling. He walked quickly, opened his arms to receive her, and give her a huge hug. They embraced for several moments before going to find her bags. Then he took her out to his new truck.

"What happened?" Noemi asked as they walked.

"I did not know that you were flying standby. I stayed for an hour after your flight landed, but you were not here. I went to every American Airlines gate, but your name was on none of their lists. I thought I was stupid to think a woman from Argentina would come to see me, so I left." Tom chuckled, "You know, when I got your page, I was at the car dealership buying a new truck. I was on my way to Montana. I'm sorry that you had such a difficult time, but I thought there was no Noemi."

"Don't worry; I will calm down in a minute." She complimented his shiny new Ranger, and they climbed in the cab. Noemi kissed Tom's cheek, then took his hand as he merged into the traffic on the way back to Denton.

Denton, Texas, USA

Tom decided that Noemi had experienced enough stress for one day, so instead of taking her back to his apartment, he headed for a La Quinta.

Inside the room, Noemi said, "I think I will take a shower if that is okay. I have been touching things on the plane all day and need to clean up."

Tom replied, "Hey, no problem."

She kissed his cheek again, "I will be right back."

"I'll be waiting."

As Noemi showered, Tom paced the room, nervous as a squirrel. He stepped outside for a smoke on the hotel balcony. It was raining hard. The drops splashed down on his head as he fretted. Noemi wouldn't want to stay in a hotel for 15 days. She was going to want to see his apartment. "I'll suck it up and take her there in the morning," he promised himself.

Noemi stepped out of the bathroom, cleaned up, and feeling better. She looked around. Tom was not there. She thought, "Now I know why he wanted a motel room for the night. He wanted to abandon me here and go home. How stupid I am." Then the door opened, and Tom walked in.

Clutching her chest, Noemi gasped, "I thought you had left me."

Tom laughed and shook his head, "I would never do that. I just went outside to smoke."

Now she smiled. "Come here."

He walked across the room, where Noemi threw her arms around him and kissed his lips. They fell on the bed and made love.

After, lying close together, Noemi smiled again. "That was just the way I imagined it would be…Wonderful."

"Holy cow, that was much more than I could ever have imagined." Tom kissed her once more, and they both drifted off to sleep.

The next morning, Tom took Noemi to breakfast at IHOP, and then they climbed in Tom's truck to head home. "I must warn you; you may think it is not much. And it isn't. But I like it."

Noemi replied, "I will love it." Once they arrived, she realized she might have spoken too soon. The complex was old and worn out. He opened the door, and she walked in to look at the space. "Oh my."

Tom shrugged, "I know, but I like it."

She began to wander around. A small living room and kitchen sat at the front. There was a single bedroom down the hall, with a big bed for Tom, and a small one where Eric had slept. Then a tiny bathroom. She returned to the front, where Tom was waiting. She said, "Okay."

"Do you mind staying here?"

"Not at all. It's not the Sheraton, but it's where you live, and I want to be with you."

Together they began to unpack her bags. Before they knew it, it was 7 p.m. Suddenly; Tom looked up. "Oh, no! I am so upset."

"Why, Baby?" Noemi looked worried.

"Because it is 7 p.m., and Noemi is not on Messenger." They laughed together, and he went on, "I'll bet you are hungry. I know I am. What kind of food do you like?"

"I like everything, but my favorite is pasta."

"Pasta, it is." The closest decent place was Olive Garden in the town of Lewisville, so together, they drove the 20 miles. On the way, Noemi held Tom's hand and constantly glanced over at him. Sometimes he would glance back and catch her gaze. Each time, he smiled and squeezed her hand.

At the restaurant, Tom arranged to have the waiter bring one of the decorative flower arrangements to their table. The waiter set them in front of her, saying, "For our Argentine lady. Welcome to the United States." Tom enjoyed watching his beautiful Noemi's face light up. They enjoyed a wonderful meal, then returned to the apartment and made love again.

In the morning, after sex and coffee, Tom looked at Noemi's happy and relaxed expression. Regretfully, he broke the bad news. He had to go to work. She smiled sadly, assuring him that she understood. He dressed, ate breakfast, and hugged her tightly. "I hate to leave you, but I have to work."

"Don't worry, I understand. I will be fine." Another kiss and Tom was off.

Alone at Tom's home, Noemi decided to take a walk in the large, beautiful park across the street. As she explored, she thought, "He must really trust me, I could steal everything in his apartment, including all of his silver coins and head back to Argentina. Tonight, I will tell him that I love him and want to marry him." Then she walked back to try and do something about that messy apartment.

Meanwhile, Tom was having a terrible day. How could he have left Noemi at the apartment alone? Why did he keep doing this job? Hadn't he done it for long enough? At that very moment, he decided that it was time for him to retire. He drove to the Sonic office, in Arlington, where he had a little meeting with the owner and gave him the news. The owner asked, "Right now?"

"Yes," Tom replied, "I cannot do this any longer." They shook hands and thanked each other for many good years. Then Tom drove home.

He found Noemi lying on the sofa, looking at the ceiling. She squealed and jumped to her feet, then ran to give him a passionate kiss. "Baby, what are you doing here so soon?"

"I thought of you here alone, and I could not stand it, so I decided to retire today."

Astonished, Noemi replied, "You would do that for me?"

"Of course! Would you like me to show you my town now that I am free?"

"Yes, I would love that. Now Noemi's face became serious. "But first, I must tell you something."

That worried Tom; that's normally not a good sentence to hear. He braced himself. Then Noemi bubbled, "I love you, Baby."

"Do you know what? I love you too."

Noemi shook her head, "No, you don't understand…I want to marry you. I love everything about you except for where you live. I love your face, I love your character, and I love everything about you."

Tom was stunned, "Wow. Are you sure?"

"I have never been surer of anything in my life. I feel great being with you, and I want to spend my life with you."

"Well, let me think about that for a while…"Tom started, and then burst out, "Yes, I would love that too. I feel great around you, and I can honestly say that I have never felt so loved."

Noemi took Tom's hand and dragged him to the bedroom. It was as if they agreed getting married is better than okay. After, Tom lookedaround the bedroom. "You changed a few things in here."

"I hope it is okay. Do you mind?"

"I love it." Noemi showed Tom the other small changes she had made. A rose in a vase in the bathroom. A tidy living room. A clean kitchen.

Tom said, "Oh my gosh. It looks great. Thank you, these changes made a huge difference." He looked into her eyes, kissed her lips, and whispered, "You are great."

She whispered back, "I love you." Then they went to see the sights of Denton.

She loved the downtown area, especially the 150-year-old courthouse. As they drove around, they talked about the future.

Tom asked, "When do you think you want to get married?"

"I don't know. I will have to go home and settle all of my affairs. Then I will return, and we can decide."

"Actually, that sounds great to me."

"This is happening just the way I dreamed about it. You are perfect," Noemi replied.

"Not so perfect," Tom said, "But very happy. You make me feel like a man who has come back to life."

The rest of the visit was beautiful. They did everything together. They made love each day, sometimes twice a day. They talked. They shared everything. Just like online, only better.

Then the day came for Noemi to return to Argentina. On the way to the airport, she held his hand tightly and told him how deeply she loved him. As he carried her bags inside, she promised, "I'm not exactly sure when, because I have much to do, but I will be back as soon as possible."

They sat together in the terminal, and Noemi cried as Tom held her, telling her that everything would be okay, and they would be together soon. They agreed to chat every night at 7 p.m., just like before. Then it was time for her to head to her gate. As they stood, she threw her arms around Tom's neck, and they kissed as if they were all alone. A passing guy even gave Tom a thumbs up. She walked through the security point, and as she walked out of sight, they waved good-bye and blew kisses to each other.

Walking to her gate, Noemi cried her beautiful eyes out. Several people stopped to ask if she was ok, and each time she would sob, "No, I'm not." She only managed to calm herself once she had plopped into her seat on the plane. Staring out the window, she sighed, thinking, "Now comes the difficult part. I hope Tom is okay until I return."

Tom watched Noemi as she walked through security and down into the terminal. Then...she was gone. Tom felt strange, helpless as a little boy. He made his way back to the truck, thinking, "Dang, as quickly as she arrived here, she has disappeared." He felt so alone that it was almost as though she had died. As he drove back to Denton, Tom's eyes were full of tears.

5
Tired of Waiting for You

Buenos Aires, Argentina

The flight went more quickly than Noemi could have hoped. After the tears had dried, dinner, and a nap on the plane, she felt hopeful insteadof heartbroken. At the airport, Pablo was waiting.

"How did it go? What was he like?"

"I have fallen in love with Tom. He's a good man, and I think we'll be happy together. I like Denton…but I didn't like his apartment. For a man who makes so much money, he lives so simply."

"Never mind his apartment. Tell me more about him."

Noemi described Tom's career, his sons, and his personality. "He has a very good character. I love him, and you will, too," she insisted.

"Now what"?

"We are going to get married."

Pablo turned to his mother in surprise, "Married? You just met him!"

"Pablo, I have chatted with him every day for almost six months, and now I have spent two weeks with him. I know more about Tom than most people know about someone in a full year. We are very comfortable and relaxed around one another. It seems like I have knownhim all of my life." She explained their plans to get married in the Statesafter settling all of her unfinished business.

At last, Pablo agreed, "Well, I trust your feelings. And I'm happy for you." He gave her a big hug and carried her luggage to the car.

Denton, Texas, USA

At home alone, Tom sat in his apartment with no Noemi to talk to. It finally hit him. He didn't work anymore. Eric was who knows where. And Noemi had a lot to do before she could come back. "Dang, I've got to find something to do with my life," he said.

For a few days, he concentrated on his eBay store. He spent his days carefully sorting rolls of Silver Eagles, handling each one with white gloves. He packed the good ones in groups of 1-12 and sent them off for grading. Silver Eagles are generally uncirculated, which means they are untouched by the general public. A coin in perfect mint state, or MS, would be graded ms70. The higher the grade, the higher the value of the coin.

It had been difficult going in the beginning. Tom would spend $7-8 per coin. Then the grading company charged him $25 to evaluate each one, plus shipping costs of $3-4. Many of his early coins received ratings as low as ms64. He expected to lose money on some of the early batches. But soon, he was regularly getting back coins with ms68 and ms69 ratings. He knew he was onto something when he spent $356 to buy and grade a group of 11 coins, then turned around and sold them for a total of $753.

Tom kept learning as he went on. He was the only vendor to sell graded coins. He figured out the most popular coin dates with buyers and honed his grading skills so he could tell the better coins on sight. Soon, he was getting back ms69 ratings almost every time. He developed a repeat customer base, and some of his regulars would contact him directly to ask if he would find particular dates for them. Sometimes he would sell to them directly and save on the eBay fees. By the days of Noemi's visit, Tom's business had become quite successful.

But now it wasn't enough. Tom often found himself bored and lonely. When they resumed their 7 p.m. chats, Noemi urged him to find something to do with his free time, like a sport. Maybe tennis?

Tom had no interest in tennis, but sitting in his apartment one day, he suddenly remembered the fun he and his friend Michael had playinggolf in junior high. They had both been terrible, but it had still been a good time. He decided to give it a try the very next day.

Tom: Today, I bought a membership at the golf course. Then I bought some clubs at a pawn shop.
Noemi: What does that mean? Will you play golf?
Tom: Yes. I played today. I wasn't very good. The ball only went 10 feet on my first swing. It took me nine shots to finish the first hole. I bought a one-year membership. Now I can play anytime I want.
Noemi: What is a set of clubs?
Tom: Ha-ha. A bag with golf clubs in it.
Noemi: Okay. I have seen golf before, and I know what you are talking about now.
Do you like golf?
Tom: I played terrible today, and I hit the ball all over the place, but I enjoyed it very much.
Noemi: I knew that you would find something to occupy your time.

Banfield, Argentina

Noemi, on the other hand, had plenty to keep her occupied. The day she returned to work; she informed her bosses that she was ready to retire. This wouldn't be as easy for her as it had been for Tom. Negotiations for an early retirement settlement were likely to take weeks or months. She was incredibly nervous about telling her supervisor, so nervous in fact that she called Tom first thing that morning. Sleepily, he reminded her, "Please don't worry. They will not hurt you. All they have is words, and you are stronger than any words."

Noemi's supervisor was not happy to hear her news. But he accepted her decision and promised to get the process started, so she walked out of his office with her head held high. She kept going in to work every day, doing her job to the best of her ability as she waited to hear their offer. She often reminisced about her 32 years with the company, andthe many years her father spent there before her. Now Pablo had a job there and would be continuing the family tradition.

In addition to work, she had to deal with her apartment. To transfer ownership to Pablo, she would have to fill out a lot of paperwork and fill it out with care.

That, however, was easy compared to dealing with her friends. They worried about the idea of this big move, which seemed risky. They had never met the man. Was it safe? Was she ready to give up her life here? They made many arguments:

"This is stupid. You're rushing into it."

"Why did you go there? Why couldn't he come to visit you here?"

"You don't know anything about him!"

All Noemi could do was reassure them she knew what is in her heart and that she trusts her instincts concerning him. Eventually, some of her friends came to accept her decision, though others would not stop trying to change her mind. During their chats, Tom cheered on Noemi. He reassured her of his feelings and told her not to let them get her down.

Tom: How was your visit with the girls?
Noemi: At first, they were not happy at all that I will be moving to Texas, but eventually, all but two of them became excited.
Tom: What about the two who were not excited?
Noemi: It's not important. They will have to take time to get used to the idea.
Tom: So, we both had a very good day!
Noemi: Yes, but now the difficult part of my time here begins.
Tom: Oh, you mean tomorrow with your bosses?
Noemi: Yes. I do not look forward to beginning that process in the morning.
Tom: It will be okay. You will see it.
Noemi: You do not know how these people are. It will not be easy.
Tom: Think of me here waiting for you, and all will be okay.
Tom: Hello. How was your day?
Noemi: It was great, and I am glad it is over.
Tom: And?
Noemi: It was very short. I told my boss, and he was not happy but said that he would begin the process.
Tom: What does that mean to begin the process?
Noemi: "Remember, this is Argentina. He will present the early retirement to the French people, and the decision will be up to them. It won't be easy.
   We will see what happens.
Noemi: How was your golf today?
Tom: Ha, awful, but better than yesterday.
   I also sold three more coins today.
Noemi: And, how much each one?
Tom: Ninety-nine dollars each.
Noemi: Oh. Very good.

Denton, Texas, USA

Tom split his days between selling coins, playing golf, and Yahoo chat. It was spring in central Texas, and the morning air felt beautiful, not too hot or too cool. He would hit the course early. There were often few or no other golfers on the course, which was just the way he wanted it. He would stand on the green grass, listening to the birds, and taking in the peace and serenity. Then he would play terribly. But slowly, his score improved. His first game he had scored 130; in the next, he scored 126. Little by little, he watched the number decrease. He laughed to himself, thinking, "At this rate, I will be able to join the PGA in 17 more years."

The time dragged on, though, as he waited to hear when Noemi would return. He had expected her to give him a firm date for her retirement, but all she could say was that the "process" had started. What the heck did that mean? He began to appreciate her struggle when she shared the latest news fully.

Noemi: I finally heard from the French today.
Tom: And?
Noemi: I asked for $100,000, and they offered $30,000.
Tom: And what do you think?
Noemi: $30,000 is a joke, and I told them I would never accept it.
Tom: So now, what do you do?
Noemi: I wait. They will have more meetings before they decide and then we will see.
Tom: I know this is frustrating for you.
Noemi: It is okay. I will fight for every last cent. I will not give up.
Tom: That's my girl.

Weeks turned to months. Next, Noemi's company came back with an offer of $30,000 and the company car she had been driving.Exasperated, she reminded them that she did not need a car. Sometimes it seemed to Tom like the fight would go on and on, and that Noemi hadbeen gone forever. Occasionally, he worried that Noemi actually had no intention of coming to the United States. All he could do was hope the situation would find a resolution soon.

Then one day, Tom got a phone call that swept aside all of his other thoughts and concerns. It was one of Eric's friends, telling him that his son was in jail for driving without insurance or registration. The court hearing was tomorrow at 2 p.m. if Tom wanted to come. In a panic, Tom made plans to be there.

The next morning, Tom made his way to the county court in Fort Worth, TX. He sat in the gallery as he heard the court clerk called Eric's name. Eric stood as the judge asked, "It seems that when they stopped you, you had no proof of insurance or registration for your vehicle, is that correct?"

"Yes, sir," Eric responded.

Then Tom rose and raised his hand. When the judge acknowledged him, Tom blurted out, "Your honor, I am Eric's father, and he does have insurance. I have paid for it every single month."

The judge instructed the court clerk to call the insurance agent, and Tom felt confident that his statement would soon be verified and his son's problem resolved. He couldn't have been more wrong. On the speakerphone, for the entire courtroom to hear, his agent insisted, "Your honor, we do not insure anyone who does not have their auto- registered." Now Tom was angry and confused; he had been paying thatbill every month! He even told the judge, "Your honor, I just sent a payment last week!" This made no difference. The judge explained that driving an unregistered vehicle was against the law, that the insurance wasn't valid if the car had no registration, and set Eric's fine at
$1250.00 plus court costs. Tom had no choice but to go downstairs and

make the payment so they would release Eric from jail. "What is happening to my son?" he wondered.

A few minutes later, Eric came out, looking depressed and embarrassed. "Let's go home," Tom told him.

"Dad, I have a home and a job here."

"You can get another job in Denton. Right now, you need to come home with me so that we can put your life back together." Eric didn't argue.

Eric was that quiet even until he saw Tom logging on to Yahoo at 7 p.m. "Are you still talking to that woman?" He scoffed.

Tom decided to ignore the tone and attitude. He just wanted to talk to Noemi. As soon as she typed, "Hello Baby," he described how tough his day had been.

Noemi: Where is Eric now?
Tom: He is here. I talked him into coming home.
Noemi: Oh my. Is everything alright?
Tom: Not yet, but it will be.
Noemi: I hope so, for your sake.
Tom: Don't worry.
How was your day?
Noemi: I still have not heard anything yet.
Tom: Do you still want to come here?
Noemi: What? Why would you ask that?
Tom: I don't know. It's been months now, and I thought you might have changed your mind.
Noemi: No. I have not changed my mind. This is stressing me out too. I work every day and wait for an answer, and this is making me very tired.

> Tom: Yes, I know. I am very tired also, so I thought I would ask to make sure you still wanted to come.
>
> Noemi: Yes, I do. It will not be much longer now. We must be a little more patient.

After signing off, Tom felt guilty. He thought, "What a day. I cannot put pressure on Noemi that way. I know she is working hard to get here." He knew it must be the stress over Eric. Tom didn't know what to do with him. And it was not a question he could answer in one night.

Banfield, Argentina

Getting ready for bed, Noemi thought about Tom's situation and how difficult things must be. If only she could be there to help. She promised herself, "I will have to put a little pressure on the French tomorrow." With that, Noemi went to bed and quickly fell asleep.

6
Back in Your Arms Again

Tom: Hello. You are early today.
Noemi: Oh, Baby. It happened. They made me a generous offer today, and I accepted it.
Tom: You are kidding me.
Noemi: No, I am not kidding. I went in today, and I insisted on meeting with the French. They said ok, but it would have to be at 2 p.m. I was planning to tell them it has been six months, and it is time to decide because this is getting ridiculous. When the meeting started, they spoke first. They offered me $55,000, and I can leave immediately.
Tomorrow morning, we will sign the papers, and the money will be transferred to my account tomorrow afternoon.
Tom: So, tomorrow you will be finished?
Noemi: Yes, sir, I will be finished. It is hard to believe; I am free now.
Tom: What a surprise. I know that makes you very happy.
Noemi: Oh, yes, I am very relieved.
Tom: So, what does all of this mean?
Noemi: I was thinking about ten days from tomorrow, does that sound okay?
Tom: Wow. Ten days, why so long?

> Noemi: I have many things to do. I have to have a
> meeting with my friends and a party with my
> coworkers. Then I must decide what things to bring
> with me. I have many things.
> Tom: I can tell you that you are excited, and that is a lot
> for you to do.
> Noemi: Yes, it is, but we will be together very soon to
> begin our new adventure.
> Tom: After all the waiting, it seems so sudden.
> Noemi: That is the Argentina way.

Denton, Texas, USA

After signing off for the evening, Tom sat in a daze. He couldn't believe he would see the woman he loved in just 10 days. He was nervous, too. After all the waiting, things were suddenly happening fast. He thought about his past, about the other marriages, and about how they ended. "All those other marriages…work got in the way every time. Well, now,I am retired. I have to pay attention to Noemi. I have to give her more attention than I've ever given a wife before. This has to work."

Banfield, Argentina

Noemi woke the next morning with a smile on her face. Joyfully, she drove to work and signed the papers that started her retirement. She called around to her friends and co-workers to give them the good news and made plans to meet up with everyone before her big move. And at 2:30 p.m. she checked her account. The money was there. Everything was falling into place, and soon she would be with Tom for the rest of her life.

For the first time since he had helped his mother open Tom's photo, Pablo began to worry. He was excited for his mother, but he wasnervous, too. For the first time in his life, she wouldn't be around. He began pestering her with questions—who was this guy who was taking her away from him? Noemi agreed that it would be a good idea for Pablo to come to visit during his next vacation, with Tom's approval, of course.

The next week flew by. There was a going-away party with 30 girlfriends of hers. There was plenty of laughter, tears, memories, and yes, some warnings that this move might be a big mistake. There was also a party with her work colleagues, many of whom she had knownfor years. It, too, was a mix of happiness and sadness. Many of her employees were worried about who the new boss would be. But the restaurant rang with laughter, and all had a great time.

The next thing she knew, Noemi had only four days left, and she hadn't even started to think about what to pack.

Denton, Texas, USA

In Texas, things weren't going quite as smoothly. Tom's coin business was running well enough. He still enjoyed golf and was getting just a little better every time he played. Plus, Eric had managed to find a job.A friend of his had taken him on as a welding apprentice and was teaching him the trade. But his son was not too happy about the Noemi situation. Unlike Pablo, Eric did not feel comfortable letting his dad follow his heart. He knew that his life would change when Noemiarrived drastically, and he didn't know what that meant. To him, shewas a total stranger.

But Tom tried not to upset Noemi with his worries. When she called a few days before her arrival, he focused on the positive.

"Hello, Baby. I could not wait until 7 pm. I wanted to hear your voice."

"Oh my, what a surprise. How are you this morning?"

"Great. I had my reunion last night, and all of my obligations are complete. Now I only have to think of what to bring. Are you ready for me?"

"I am ready for you completely," Tom assured her, "Remember, if you forget something, Pablo can bring it when he comes.

"Oh, I did not think of that. Now I can pack without stress."

"Leave the stress in Argentina. I was thinking about how much has happened in the past seven or so months. A lot."

"Yes. And now we will be together in a few days. I am excited to be with you again."

"You are not nearly as excited as I am."

"I need to go buy a suitcase for the trip. I may need to buy two or three."

Tom looked around his tiny apartment, concerned. "Sounds like you're bringing a lot of things."

"Yes. I have a lot of things that I don't want to leave here."

"Well, take your time and have fun with it. I will chat with you at 7 pm."

"Thank you. I will. I love you."

"I love you. Bye for now."

Tom: "Hello, Noemi. It was great to hear your voice this morning. How was your day"?
Noemi: Busy. I bought three new suitcases and was able to pack two of them today. Now, I only have five more to go.

Tom: Wow. You are bringing seven bags?
Noemi: Yes. I hope I don't need to buy more.
Tom: Do you know what?
Noemi: No. What?
Tom: After today, you only have three days left.
Noemi: Time is moving very fast for me. How about you"?
Tom: No. Time is not moving as fast for me, but you will be here before we know it.
Noemi: Yes, but not too soon for me.
Tom: Ha. Or too soon for me.

Buenos Aires, Argentina

And Tom was right. Before she knew it, Noemi was in Pablo's car, heading to the airport. They had to call an extra taxi for her seven massive bags. When he started to complain, she gave him the stare. "This isn't a vacation, it's a move," she reminded him. Wisely, Pablo said no more about it.

DFW Airport, USA

This time, when Tom arrived at the airport, he didn't have long to wait. He had awoken that morning with the thought, "Today's the day." Aday when the lives of people he cared about would change. The morning had gone by incredibly slowly, but now he was waiting outside the gate. And there she was. She stepped into his arms, and they hugged for a long time, oblivious to everyone around them.

They held hands as they walked to the baggage claim. When he saw the number and size of her suitcases, he quickly agreed to hire a skycap.

Traffic on the way home was terrible, but Noemi held Tom's hand the whole way, and neither of them noticed the delays.

When they arrived at the apartment, Eric was waiting outside. He looked into the bed of the truck and exclaimed, "That is a lot of bags!" They laughed together, and then Eric headed out to visit a friend. He promised to be home by 10 p.m. and was gone.

Alone, at last, Noemi and Tom fell into each other's arms and made love for the first time in many long months. Afterward, as they lay together, Tom sighed, "Finally, it is over."

Noemi smiled and said, "Actually, it is just beginning."

"True that," said Tom.

7
The Long Road Home

Denton, Texas, USA

The next few days were quiet. They took care of ordinary things like opening a new bank account for Noemi's retirement savings. Often, she sat and watched Tom as he managed his coin business, shipping orders, taking e-mail requests from customers, and managing his eBay store. "Looks like fun!" she said.

"Yes. And it's easy, too!"

They also talked about the future. Neither of them felt sure what to do with their lives next, and they agreed to keep it simple: sell coins, take a trip to Montana, and spend as much time together as possible.

Tom was also quietly watching Eric, and seeing that these were not happy days for his son. This wasn't surprising; even though Eric was a young man instead of a small boy, it was hard for him to accept the presence of a new woman in the house. And he didn't much like sleeping in the living room, either. Tom and Noemi decided it would be best for everyone if they set off on their trip sooner rather than later.

So, they bought a map (these were the days before GPS) and set out for Montana.

Taos County, NM

They chose a route that would lead them through New Mexico. Neither of them had ever been there, and the two were pleasantly surprised to find themselves in the Rocky Mountains. Looking down from a summit with a beautiful scenic overlook, without even realizing it, they both fell in love. Stopping for a break in Durango, Colorado, Noemi turned to Tom and said. "This is nice, but I liked that area near Taos."

Tom smiled and replied, "Then let's go back." They turned right around and made a five-hour drive back the way they had come. Arriving in the area, Tom pulled over and asked, "Now what?"

Noemi pointed at a nearby cabin. "Why don't we knock on their door? We can ask if they know of any nearby places for sale.

"Good idea."

The elderly lady who answered looked a little confused to see them, but when she heard what they wanted, she suggested they head up the road to a local store. "Just before the Sipapu ski resort," she said, "They are friends of mine, and their daughter would likely know of anything that may be for sale."

When they arrived at the store, Tom and Noemi laughed to discover they'd already passed it three times in their travels. They told the owner, a middle-aged lady with red hair, about their conversation with the elderly lady. "That's Mattie," she nodded, and she agreed to call her daughter Emily to drive over and help out with finding local cabins for sale. While she was on the phone, snow began to fall. Noemi watched it through the window. "It's beautiful," she sighed, "But it could be dangerous if there's much more." Outside, the highway was beginningto turn white.

Hanging up the phone, the store owner replied, "Don't worry. This won't amount to anything. Every year around this time, we get quick, afternoon snows. Then it stops, and all is well. It's the deep winter you have to worry about around here. In the winter, it snows by the foot, sometimes up to two hundred and fifty inches."

Tom raised his eyebrows, "Wow, that's quite a bit."

"Yep, it can get pretty hairy at times."

At that moment, Emily walked in the door. She appeared to be in her late twenties, plump, with hair that looked as if it hadn't undergone brushing in a couple of weeks. She wore multiple layers of clothing, with a ski jacket, a scarf, and an Indiana Jones-type hat pulled down low over her eyes. When Tom shook her hand, it was rough and cold. She offered to drive them around and show them some cabins, so they all piled into Emily's SUV.

Over the hill, they went past a row of mailboxes to a dusty road. The sign above it read, "Valle Del Rito." They crossed the cattle guard, headed up the rough and bumpy trail, turned left at a fork, and crossed over an old, rickety bridge. At last, they arrived at a row of cabins.Emily pointed to an A-frame building straight up the hill. "That's the one."

"How the heck are you going to get up that hill?" Tom asked, "It must be forty yards straight up!"

Emily laughed as she said, "I have four-wheel drive." Sure enough, the SUV easily did the climb. She pulled to a stop at the front door, and they all spotted the padlock. "Uh oh, I'd better call Ermo. He looks after the property for Mr. Richardson, who lives in Tucumcari." Emily said she'd go to her cabin to make the call and promised to be back as soon as she could. Tom and Noemi waited, wondering if Emily's place was anything like this one.

Ermo arrived in a beat-up old truck that came screaming down the dusty road and then zipped up the hill. He had a pair of bolt cutters in hand. Only Mr. Richardson had a key, so Ermo wrestled with the old padlock for a few minutes. At last, they heard it snap, then Ermo opened the door, and followed them inside.

Tom and Noemi looked around in wonder. The floor plan was open, and the living room gave way to the kitchen. The furniture was old and worn out, but the kitchen had everything, including dishes and silverware and pots and pans. Up a spiral staircase lay an open, loft-style bedroom. They looked over the rail down into the living room, and then out the four triangular windows across the way. The view was spectacular.They could see the road, the bridge, the highway, and a mountainside covered with pine and aspen trees. Noemi said, "Oh, Baby. It's beautiful."

As Tom stared in awe, "Yes, it is."

As they walked out, Ermo quoted the asking price—$90,000—and gave them Mr. Richardson's contact information. He grabbed his bolt cutters from the deck and was gone as fast he had arrived. Emily offered to show them another cabin. She pointed down the road, "But I'll have to go there and make another phone call first." They all piled back into her SUV.

They bumped back down the trail and over the rickety bridge; Emily pulled up in front of a barren, run-down looking place. She led them inside. The interior was worse than the exterior. Ugly, brown vinyl covered the floors. Trash lay everywhere. The cabinets had chicken wire fronts, like rabbit cages. The smell was terrible, and Noemi's stomach started to churn. She tried to hold her breath.

At last, Emily finished her call, and they stepped back into the fresh air. Noemi and Tom exchanged a look that asked, "How do people live like this?" They couldn't wait to get away.

The second place was not nearly as impressive as the A-frame. It was a square box with a bed against one wall and a recliner against the other, with a wood-burning stove between them. There was no real kitchen, just a hotplate, and a tiny refrigerator in a corner. The small window above the sink did have a beautiful view, but that was the only good thing Noemi could see. "How do people live in a space so small?" she asked.

Emily giggled. "This is a summer cabin. People don't live here all year. They just come for the summer. There is no insulation in the walls so that you couldn't stay in winter."

"No thanks," Noemi said and walked out.

Tom shrugged at Emily. "I guess we're not interested in this one."

After they had said goodbye to Emily, Tom and Noemi agreed to head straight back to Texas, stopping in at Tucumcari, NM, to make Mr. Richardson an offer. In the truck, they talked at length about theiroptions. $90,000 seemed a little high. Plus, there would be a need for new furniture, kitchenware, and household goods to decorate the place. They did the math on their funds: Noemi had received $55,000 from the French company. Tom had $60,000 tied up in Silver Eagles, another $20,000 in cash, and another $10,000 in other silver coins. Altogether, they had $145,000 available. They should be able to manage it.

Their conversation made the time go by quickly, and before they knew it, they were sitting in front of Mr. Richardson's house. It was anaverage size place in an average neighborhood. This surprised them, as Ermo had said his boss had been a politician and state representative before he had retired. They squeezed each other's hands, walked up the path to the door, and took a deep breath. Noemi crossed her fingers as Tom rang the bell.

The older woman was surprised to see two strangers at her door, and even more surprised when Tom said, "Hello, I'm Tom, and this isNoemi. We just looked at your cabin in Taos County this morning, and we would like to talk with you about purchasing it." Even so, sheinvited them inside and led them into the den. Her husband sat there in arecliner, watching college football on TV.

He was frail and sickly looking, with thinning hair, but his face opened in a wide smile. He shook their hands. Tom explained, "We certainly don't mean to bother you and interrupt your game, but we looked atyour cabin in Taos County this morning. We wanted to talk with you about buying it. Ermo showed us around, and Noemi fell in love withit."

Mr. Richardson did not mince words. In a gruff voice, he replied, "Well, I need $90,000 for it, and I will not take a penny less."

"We have $50,000 in cash today, but the remainder is in silver," Tom replied. "I would need a little time to liquidate it. So, if you would accept $50,000 now and $40,000 in six months, I believe we could make a deal today."

Mr. Richardson was silent for a moment. Then he shook his head. "You seem like nice people. But I can't do that. I need cash. You see, I'm old and not in very good health, and I am trying to tie up loose ends for my wife in case I don't live much longer. If I sell that cabin, I must have $90,000 in cash."

Tom nodded sadly. He gave Mr. Richardson his phone number, in case he changed his mind, and they said their goodbyes. When they got to the truck, Noemi looked at Tom with tears in her eyes. Her voice shook as she said, "Baby, I wanted that cabin. Is there anything we can do?"

"I loved it too, but the truth is that the cabin will take most of our cash. We have a long drive back to Texas, so there's plenty of time to talk about it." They found a motel room and turned in for the night. Both hadhad tears in their eyes as they fell asleep.

The next day, all their conversation revolved around the A-frame and how much they had loved it. Noemi talked endlessly about the beautiful view through the windows. Tom wondered aloud about the wisdom of spending all their cash to buy it.

Denton, Texas, USA

When they arrived at Tom's apartment, Eric was surprised to see them back so soon. Tom took him aside and quietly explained what had happened.

"Now what?" Eric wanted to know.

"Not sure," Tom shook his head.

Fortunately, Noemi pushes aside her disappointment quickly as she prepared for Pablo's visit. At one point, in the middle of her happy preparations, she said to Eric, "Pablo arrives tomorrow. Are you ready?"

Eric grumbled, "I guess. I don't have a choice, do I?"

Noemi didn't know how to respond, but she promised, "It will bealright. Pablo is a good boy, and you will like him."

At the airport, seeing Pablo for the first time, Tom was surprised to see he was a big man. He was even more surprised when Pablo kissed him on both cheeks after hugging Noemi. But Tom went with the flow.

Like Pablo's mother, Pablo was surprised by the size and age of his apartment, and once again, Tom felt a little embarrassed. But they did their best to make him feel at home. Before long, Eric arrived, and now the place seemed small. After dinner, they decided Pablo would sleep on the floor in the living room, where Eric was already occupying the sofa. Tom's son was unhappy about this, and the whole place seemed smaller still.

Pablo enjoyed exploring the town that was his mother's new home. He walked alone across the park and through the old downtown area. He watched the people and thought about how everything compared to what he had seen on visits to New York and California. He toured Texas Stadium with Tom and Noemi, where they were allowed to walk on the field of the Dallas Cowboys. One of the tour guides even teed up a football at the twenty-yard line, and Pablo put the ball through the uprights, which may have been the most exciting part of his visit. Then came the sad day of his departure, and they had lunch at the airport together after checking Pablo's bags. While their laughter resonated throughout the restaurant, the tears began to flow as the time neared for Pablo's plane to leave. As they approached the security area, Noemi held Pablo in her arms as only a mother could. Then Pablo turned to hug Tom, and to whisper in his ear, "You are a good man, please take care of my mother." Tom nodded yes, and then Pablo disappeared into the crowd. Tom turned to Noemi and promised her that they would travel to Argentina at least once each year to visit with him. That thought gave Noemi strength as they headed for home.

With Pablo gone, Tom and Noemi realized that they were no closer to a cabin than when Noemi first arrived in Denton. "What if we went back to that area and looked again? Maybe there is something else in the neighborhood," Tom suggested. They agreed to get in touch with Mattie first, and she gave them a number for her friend Theresa.

When they called, Theresa was cautious. "Well, there is one place." She warned them, "The man who owns it is very difficult to work with, but he may want to sell." She gave Tom the contact information.

Once he hung up the phone, he turned to Noemi and said, "Well, cross your fingers. We have a lead." He dialed the number and explained to the man who answered what they were looking for.

Don, the owner, quickly responded, "Well, yes, that cabin is for sale. I'm asking $50,000 for it. At the moment, it is rented, but the woman has not paid any rent in more than a year. So, it should not be a problem getting her out. If you would like to see it, I will give you the address, and you can drive by, then call me back, and we can talk about it."

When Tom hung up the phone, he asked Noemi, "Are you ready for another trip to Taos?"

Noemi hugged him, saying, "I'm ready to go right this minute."

Tom laughed, "Slow down a little; we can leave in the morning."

"Okay, I think I can wait that long."

Taos County, NM

It was a 10-hour drive, but they chatted about how beautiful Taos County was and how they hoped this would turn out to be "The Place." Their excitement built and built, and eventually, they turned down the dusty road under the Valle Del Rito sign. They scanned the cabins, looking for number 17. They found cabin number 11, then number 13, and then cabin number 15...something began to look uncomfortably familiar. Before they reached number 17, Noemi shrieked and squealed, "No. Lord, please. No." Tom brought the truck to a stop. There they were in front of Emily's dumpy house. It bore the number 17.

Noemi howled, "I cannot believe this. This is the worst house I have ever seen. What a waste of time." Tom just sat there silent, in shock, wondering what to say to her. Eventually, they decided that since they had driven so far, they might as well walk around.

They could tell Emily was not home, so they wandered slowly around the outside. The roof was new, metal, and the nicest part of the exterior. However, the stones of the fireplace were starting to separate from the cabin wall by four inches or more. And they both remembered how the inside looked. They turned the truck around and sped back to Texas in disgust.

But on the way home, Tom began to think a little more deeply. Maybe this was an opportunity in disguise. He convinced Noemi to let him talk to Don, regardless of the cabin's current condition. He made the call as soon as they got home.

"Hello Tom, how are you today?"

"Not so good, Don. We just got back from Taos, where we looked at your place. We were very disappointed."

"Why? What was wrong?"

"How long has it been since you have been there?"

"About three years."

"Ok, Don. I cannot pay $50,000 for that place. The inside is in awful condition and smells terrible. Noemi got sick while we were there. The outside is falling apart, and the chimney is pulling away from the cabin."

Don was quiet for a while. Finally, he asked, "Well, Tom, how much would you offer for my cabin?"

Tom didn't even think about his response. "Thirty-five thousand," spilled out of his mouth.

Don thought some more, then said, "It's been several years since I have been there because I am in bad health and can't travel to Taos to inspect the cabin. I will have to take your word for it that the place is a mess. Okay, Tom, thirty-five thousand it is."

After hanging up, Tom turned excitedly to Noemi and said, "We have our cabin."

"I hate that place," she confessed.

Tom hugged her and said gently, "It's a great deal, much better than ninety thousand dollars. We can do something with it."

The next phase took weeks. It seemed that every time Tom spoke to Don, the man would change his mind and decide not to sell his cabin. Then the next day, he would be ready to sell again. This behavior drove Tom crazy for more than a month until, at last, Emily got evicted, and the closing date for the cabin was set.

They drove to New Mexico for the closing, taking a mattress in the bed of the truck. When they arrived, the cabin was a mess. Emily had left piles of trash everywhere as she made her exit. Noemi quickly got busy cleaning so they could stand being in the place during the night. Once nightfall came, they settled onto the mattress to sleep, and the wind began to kick up. It howled in at what seemed like 80 miles an hour. Snow began to fall. Each time a car passed on the highway close by, Noemi would wake. Each time, she thought she saw the silhouette of a bear outside. Eventually, they realized that it was only a shadow of a tree limb that she saw.

In the morning, they woke up exhausted and went outside to find eight inches of snow. They decided to take a walk before driving into Taos to sign the last papers. As they hiked beneath the trees, Noemi began to cry. "Baby, I don't think I can live here. The place is nasty and awful, and the weather is more than I expected."

Tom took her in his arms. "I think we can fix this."

"What do you mean, fix this?"

"We can remodel this cabin, and you will fall in love with it."

Noemi had doubts about Tom's remodeling skills, but she agreed, "Okay. We will try." Then they headed to the city of Taos to close the deal, where they paid the thirty-five thousand dollars and the closing costs. They were handed the papers and told that the deal would not officially close until Don signed them, so Tom and Noemi agreed todrop by Weatherford, TX, on their way back to Denton.

Weatherford, TX

They set out the next morning. Weatherford was 40 miles away from Denton, so they made the long drive, and then spent more time trying to locate Don's house. It was not an easy place to find, but at last, they pulled up to the trailer with the right address. A woman sat on the porch, watching them climb down from the truck. She called out, "You must be Tom and Noemi. I'm Sarah, Don's girlfriend. He is inside."

They followed her in to discover a place almost as trashy as Emily's. They had to step over junk on their way to Don's bedroom, and just like the cabin, the smell was almost unbearable. Don himself was in bed.

After they shook hands, Tom asked, "Ready to go?"

"Yes, but can you help me with my walker?" For the next few minutes, Tom struggled to help Don stand and make his way to the walker. The trip to the front door took even longer, as Tom had to move many items on the floor out of Don's way. Finally, slowly, Don made it down the ramp of the trailer and to Tom's truck.

As they drove to the notary's office for the final signing, Don asked, "How much money will I get?"

Tom had been dreading this moment. He had to explain what the bank had told him. "Well, Don, I'm afraid you will not receive any cash. You owed some unpaid income tax and property tax. There's nothing left after settling those." He held his breath. After three months of flip- flopping, he was afraid that Don would back out of the deal. But to his surprise, Don just nodded. They got to the notary's office and signed with no problems. Suddenly, Tom and Noemi owned a cabin in the middle of The Carson National Forrest in Taos County.

On the way back to Don's trailer, he asked: "Could you please take me to Walmart so that I can buy a pair of reading glasses?"

"No problem," said Tom.

Once there, Tom helped Don settle into a scooter. To his and Noemi's surprise, the man began going isle to isle, filling his basket. They followed him to the cashier and watched a lady ring up his purchases. Then Don exclaimed, "Shit. I left my money at home." He looked up at Tom. "Could you get this for me?"

Tom was not a happy camper, but he didn't argue. Instead, he just paid the bill, and the three made their way back to the truck. Soon, Don was delivered back to his trailer, and after all the thank yous and goodbyes, Tom and Noemi were back on the highway.

8
Little Cabin in the Woods

Denton, Texas, USA

Tom was very excited to have finally closed the deal on the cabin, and he couldn't wait to get started on the remodel. Noemi was more skeptical. "I hope we can change it enough so that we can live there," she grumbled.

Tom chuckled and squeezed her hand. "Don't worry; everything will be fine. In fact, how would you feel about going to Taos tomorrow and getting started?"

"I would love that."

"Done."

The next morning, Tom sat Eric down for a chat. "Son, Noemi, and I are moving today. We will put my stuff into storage and then travel to Taos. I'm leaving you with this apartment. I will also leave you all of the things you need like the bed, the sofa, the TV, dishes, and pots and pans. The rent is cheap enough that you can afford it. I hope that you always pay the rent on time. If not, you know what will happen."

Eric was speechless. He had known this day was coming, but he did not expect it this quickly. He watched them load Tom's things into the truck, and then they said their goodbyes and drove away. Just like that, he was on his own.

Tom was nervous as he locked 6000 Silver Eagles and several thousand other silver coins into a storage unit and drove away. But as the miles went on, and Noemi chatted excitedly about her thoughts on decor, he began to relax. She was full of ideas. This was the start of a new life.

Taos County, NM

It was late when they arrived, so Tom and Noemi crashed on the mattress they'd left on the floor. They woke up ready to go. They agreed to call in professional contractors for plumbing and electricity. And Ermo was ready and willing to help with the cabinetry. They made plans for all the construction folks to arrive the next day and Noemi concentrated on cleaning.

Sure enough, Ermo, the plumber, and the electrician arrived bright and early the following morning. Noemi did most of the talking as she led them through the house. "I want to move the stove on this side of the kitchen and the refrigerator on this side. I want a plug here and a light switch here. We need a light fixture here, and I want a dishwasher there. We will need new cabinets, countertops and new vinyl in the kitchen. Berber carpet throughout the rest of the cabin, new windows, a new staircase to the upstairs room." Everyone had their marching orders and got started the right away.

Tom and Ermo decided to cover the walls of the cabin with tongue and groove aspen. As the workers swarmed the house inside and out, crawling on ladders in the kitchen, under the kitchen sink, beneath the foundation beams, and elsewhere, Noemi began to see the possibilities. She stood back, watching, and told Tom, "It's incredible, and it will be beautiful."

Over the next weeks, Tom and Noemi went back and forth to Home Depot in Santa Fe for all new appliances, cabinets, countertops, windows, light fixtures, bathroom vanities, commodes, and a thousand other small things. Each time, they loaded up their pickup to the brim, and they headed home in the dark. There they were, two 50-year-olds in the cold, moving heavy appliances into the cabin. But Noemi was like a child at Christmas, brimming with excitement. She would look at Tom with stars in her eyes, saying, "Now, it's beginning to look like something."

Ermo helped Tom install the aspen boards and the windows, texture, and painted the ceilings, and tore down the old staircase. Then it was time for the flooring company to come in and do their job. Slowly, the nasty little hovel became a beautiful and charming place. Finally, it remained only to repair and paint the exterior. Noemi picked a color thatreminded Tom of a gingerbread house.

Then, they completed the painting. The run-down cabin had been restored to life and was a place that she could finally call home. Noemi danced through the interior and out into the front yard, crying, "I love it.I love it. I love it." She spun to Tom and said, "You were right, Baby,we could fix it, and we did. Look at this beauty; look at it!" Tom just smiled. In his eyes, the joy in Noemi's face had made everything worthwhile.

They felt so blessed and amazed at how God had entered their lives since they had met. There had been so many unexpected blessings. For example, during the long winter of remodeling, they realized that Mr. Richardson's cabin would have been snowed in, with them in it. Noemi commented, "God told us no on a frame. He said, 'I have something much better in mind for the two of you.' And He did. What a blessing."

"You know," he said, "I think that in the 17 months we have been together, we have been through more and learned more about each other than if we were together every day for 17 years."

"Absolutely!" she agreed, "I feel as though I know you better than I know anyone on this planet. Give me a kiss!" Tom gladly obliged.

As they worked on building a new life together, Tom and Noemi watched things change for their sons. First, Pablo found a new love, Laura, and she moved her into his apartment. Soon after, his first daughter popped into his life. Noemi thought being a grandmother was heaven. She always said, "If a man is thirty-five years of age, and he does not have children, he is lazy." Well, finally, she no longer considered her son lazy.

Tom's oldest son, Jeff, was recruited by a computer company for a job in Boston. His job involved designing huge computer systems for large companies like General Electric, then teaching those companies how to use those systems. A woman named Kris soon moved there to be with him. Unfortunately, Kris and Tom didn't get along. The longer they were together, the angrier Jeff began to feel about his parents' divorce. Eventually, the communication between Tom and his older son ceased.

Eric, too, was struggling. He still had issues with drugs, and his friends were not a positive influence. Tom rarely spoke to his second son, either.

Because Tom had few ties remaining in Denton, and Noemi had left behind her life in Argentina, they could think of no better place to hold their wedding than their new home. They started planning right away. There were invitations to order, catering to arrange, and a honeymoon to book, too, of course. They set a date for June 4. Noemi invited all of the neighbors: Theresa and her husband Tommy, Mattie, and Jack, and of course, Ermo. The local preacher agreed to come to conduct the ceremony at the cabin.

When the day arrived, the weather was sunny and cool. The birds were out in full force, filling the air with beautiful songs. Tom, as usual, woke up before Noemi and went to make coffee. He heard sounds from the bedroom and knew his bride was awake, so he poured her a cup of coffee with cream and headed for the bedroom. "Good morning, beautiful. How did you sleep?"

"Oh baby, I slept like a queen. I thought I would be awake all night long, but the truth is, I just woke up!" He handed her the coffee and slid into bed for a kiss.

She looked out the window. "I think today is a beautiful day to get married."

Holding her close, he looked into her eyes and said, "I love you."

"And I love you!" She gave him a long kiss before her eyes went wide. "We have to move it. The caterer will be here in less than an hour! Go, go, go. And we're not to see each other again until the ceremony." With one last kiss, she shooed him out of the room fast enough to make his head spin. He went to the kitchen to get another cup of coffee and to wait for the caterer.

Noemi was a nervous mess as she got dressed in her new bedroom, filled with new furniture, including a beautiful bed that stood three feet off the floor. She looked around, thinking, "How lucky am I to have such a place and such a man?" She knelt by the bedside, next to her dress, and prayed, "Heavenly Father, I thank you so much for this day. I thank you for Tom and all that we mean to one another. I ask that yoube with us today and throughout our marriage and give us the strength and courage that we both need to make each other happy. Thank you, Lord, In Jesus name, I pray. Amen."

Wiping away tears, she had to smile. "Here I am in a strange country, in a strange state, in a strange forest, with a strange man. Am I crazy or what?" Still, she felt this was the best decision she had ever made. With that, she began to dress.

In the living room, Tom was feeling a little melancholier as hedrank his coffee alone. He was thinking about his sons. Neither of them knew their father was getting married today. "I guess that's the price they'll have to pay for excluding me from their lives." Still, he wished things could have been different. Then he heard a knock at the door, which meant the caterer had arrived. And soon Tom was too busy forsad thoughts.

The snacks and chairs arrived, and they arranged them without any difficulties. Tom had time to put on his suit before Tommy and Theresa, the first of the guests, arrived. Theresa immediately excused herself to go to Noemi's bedroom. As he took a seat on the couch, Tommygrinned, "Looks like you're going to have a party."

Tom laughed, "Not a party. A wedding. Someone's getting married here today."

"Who could that be?"

"Guess we'll find out!"

Theresa knocked on the bedroom door. She poked her head in and saw Noemi already dressed. "You look beautiful."

"Thank you."

Theresa sat down on the bed and took Noemi's hand. "Are you nervous?"

"I have never been happier. Tom is a wonderful man, and I love him with all my heart. But I'm glad you are here. I was a mess. I don't like waiting."

The living room soon filled with 20 or more guests. They, Tom, and the preacher all anxiously waited for the moment to come. Then the music began, and Noemi entered her new living room. She was gorgeous, simply gorgeous, as she walked in the room, her face lit up like a neon sign. She made her way to the rented decorative arch, her radiant smile, giving all the guests chills. Noemi's beauty almost brought Tom to his knees. He thought, "How can I possibly deserve all of this? A beautiful woman, a gorgeous cabin in the mountains, and so many wonderful friends."

As they stood together under the arch, Noemi whispered into his ear, "I'm as nervous as hell."

He chuckled, "Me too."

They joined hands as the preacher began the ceremony, and as quickly as it had begun, it was over. Tom and Noemi were man and wife. They came together for a long, passionate kiss. When they finally parted, Tom called out, "Anyone hungry?"

Shouts of "Alright!" and "Hell, yes!" filled the room, and everyone headed for the food.

Before they knew it, people opened all the gifts, and all the food was gone. Most of the guests had gone home. Tommy and Theresa offeredto handle the cleanup and lock the cabin, so Tom and Noemi hopped in the pickup. They headed for the Angel Fire ski resort, about sixty miles away, for their honeymoon.

On the drive, Noemi asked, "What do you think?"

"I think I love you."

"No, no, I meant, what did you think about the wedding?"

Tom replied, "I thought it was beautiful."

"I did too. I loved everything about it. And aren't we lucky to have good friends to tidy up, so we don't have to come home to a mess?"

"Yep, they're good people."

They arrived at the hotel at 9 p.m., long after dark. Unfortunately, they had not considered that this was the off-season. Tom asked the front desk receptionist, "Where is the restaurant"?

"It is through this hallway, but it closes at 7 p.m. during the offseason."

Tom asked, "Where can we find an open restaurant?"

The clerk shook his head, "I don't believe there is one this time of the night. It's a small town. Just 1089 people. So, things close up early."

In the end, they had only one choice. The sole business they could find open was the local gas station. Noemi picked a microwave pizza, and Tom had a microwave burrito.

As they ate their honeymoon dinner in the car, Noemi began to laugh loudly. Tom said, "What is so funny about this mess?"

This occurrence took her a moment to calm down, but at last, she said, "All of this is so funny. As bad as this is, we will never forget this wonderful pizza and burrito."

Tom snorted, "I hope that you don't remind me of this on every anniversary." Then they laughed as they went to the hotel.

9
Do the Hustle

Taos County, NM

For a year or more, life felt like a fairy tale. Tom continued to sell coins on eBay, and Noemi soon learned enough to help him run the business. They found a beautiful golf course about forty miles from the cabin, andhe began to teach her how to play. Often, they would come home from the course to discover that they had sold five or six $500 coins and several rolls of Silver Eagles. Life was good.

Noemi started the process of applying for a green card. She did the research online and told Tom, "Attorneys want too much money to take care of the citizenship process. I think we can do it ourselves."

He looked around their beautifully remodeled cabin and replied, "You and I are pretty smart people, and I think we can do that."

"I love when you say that," she smiled.

She soon found the appropriate paperwork, they filled out the forms, and wasted no time before taking them to the post office. Noemi spent the next few weeks in a state of eager impatience before they summonedthem to Albuquerque for her first appointment. After their three-hour drive, she was fingerprinted and questioned by a naturalization agent, then told her that she would hear from them in a month or so.

Tom knew the process could take a long time, and he would often tell her, "Be patient." But Noemi could hardly stand the wait.

The same year, the state was considering a ban on the pit bull breed of dog. Suddenly, the woods around Tom and Noemi's house seemed full of dogs as people would drive to the mountains and abandon them there. They kept finding pit bulls at their door and had their hands full, trying to find homes for them. One day, while Noemi was in town for a hair appointment, a beautiful dog wandered up to the cabin. He was afraid and would not come close to Tom, so Tom went inside and fetched a handful of food. The dog gobbled it down. Then Tom created a trail of food that led through the garage and into the house. The dog followed it, and Tom shut the door after. Now it was trapped inside.

When Noemi got home, Tom was waiting outside. "I've got a dog trapped in there," he told her. "It's the most beautiful pit bull." She was surprised and a little scared. But she followed him inside, and when the dog saw her, he ran up, wagging his tail. She gave a little shriek, thinking he was attacking, but then she saw that the dog only wanted a little attention.

Tom named the dog Goober because he seemed so goofy. Then the three of them began to build a routine. Each morning Tom, Noemi, and Goober walked through their neighborhood. Goober would run free while Tom and Noemi held hands and took in the beautiful scenery. Sometimes the dog would dash back to them as if checking to make sure they were okay. Those were fun and peaceful days.

Then, suddenly, the fairytale turned dark. Tom had been the only seller of graded Silver Eagles on eBay for a long time. He could set any price he wanted, and every coin would sell without a problem. Then, other dealers realized what he was doing and began sending their coins in for grading. Some of these started their auctions as low as one cent. Coins began to sell cheap. Then the market became saturated, and the demand disappeared. Tom was out of business.

Worse, Tom's credit was in awful shape. He had not filed a tax return for six years, so he had no checking account. He paid cash for everything. With that in mind, they had put the cabin in Noemi's name. But now the IRS caught up to Tom. He got a letter stating that he owed $43,000 in back taxes. They were in shock. With their main source of income cut off and the cash in the bank dwindling, they had no idea how they would pay this new debt.

At this point, Tom also admitted to Noemi that he had no retirement plan. She was surprised and seriously worried about the future, but she decided to attack the problem with her typical determination. "First, we fix your credit," she announced.

They got a copy of his report and discovered that his score was a 530, partly because his record listed a judgment from a county tax office in Tennessee. Tom was sure he'd paid that years ago, so he called the county office and requested an investigation. They confirmed that he was correct, and within sixty days, they removed the judgment from all credit reports.

Next, he contacted the IRS. When an agent came on the line, Tom explained his situation and admitted, "I have no way to pay such a huge bill."

"How much can you pay?" the agent replied.

Tom didn't even think about his response. "Seventeen thousand," spilled out of his mouth.

"Okay," said the agent.

"But I can't pay it all at once. I have no cash and no way to borrow."

"I can put you on a payment plan. How much can you afford to pay each month?"

"I don't know, maybe $700."

"Okay, Mr. Bradburn. I can accept $700 per month for the next two years. In the meantime, file a tax return every year, and don't be late with your payments!"

When he hung up the phone and reported the news to Noemi, she felt the panic rising in her heart. "How in the world will we pay $700 per month? We need money. We have to get jobs."

For the first time in their relationship, they now had to hustle. First, Noemi searched online for jobs and found a teaching position in anearby town. As she had been an English teacher in Argentina, she thought this might be a good fit. So, she applied and was hired within a week. Unfortunately, the job ended up adding to Noemi's stress instead of solving their problems. The school was 60 miles away. She had to getout of bed at 5:30 each morning to get there on time. As if that was not bad enough, during the winter months, she had to drive over treacherousroads full of snow and ice. Her students were worse. She struggled to control their behavior, they had no respect for authority, and they began to wear her down. Then the principal called her into his office to explainthat she needed a U.S. teacher's license to keep the job. If she wanted to apply for a license, she could stay on as a substitute for lower pay until she got it.

"No, thanks," she said. She resigned on the spot and went home to Tom.

Next, Tom decided opening a restaurant might be the answer. After all, it was the thing he had done successfully for many years. Noemi didn't like the idea, but they went to Taos to ask a bank about a loan. His credit was better, thanks to their recent efforts, but not good enough.And they had no collateral. The bank declined their application.

When they got home, Noemi headed straight to the computer and her go-to source for information. Soon she came across a description for a job called "mystery shopper." It sounded like something they could do with no trouble. Companies would hire individuals to go into different kinds of retail businesses like restaurants or shoe stores. The mystery shopper's job secretly evaluates locations by studying the services, quality of the product, the cleanliness of the shop, friendliness, and professionalism of the employees, and so on.

At first, they made very little money, though they got many free meals. Then they figured out that the real money was to be made by scheduling multiple shops at once and getting reimbursed for travel expenses. Since New Mexico is such a sparsely populated state, Tom and Noemi were in great demand. They traveled the entire state, began to make hundreds of dollars per trip, and they were able to pay their bills each month, including the $700 tax bill.

The problem was that they were never home and did not get to enjoy their beautiful cabin in the Carson National Forest. They looked again, this time for something closer to home. Tom picked up some work in merchandising, which meant stocking shelves at stores like Walmart and Walgreens. But the money was lean, and Tom didn't like the idea that someone he knew would walk into Walgreens and see him sittingon the floor stocking product, and he left the job.

At last, they took to gamble. They took their last dollars and went to an auction. They bought a car, took it to the cabin, and cleaned it up. Noemi washed and detailed it, and Tom did the service on it and filled the fluids. Then they parked it out by the highway with a "for sale sign."Each morning they drove it out and parked it, and each night they brought it home. After a couple of days, they received a call, and just like that, they sold their first car and made $1,500 profit.

They were about as excited as two people could be. Noemi said, "That was so easy and fun. Let's do it again!" She loved the fast, exciting pace of the auctions. The next car they bought was a 4x4 SUV. They had the same luck, and it sold within a couple of days.

The couple went to auctions in Denver, Dallas, and Albuquerque, and had soon bought and sold a total of fifteen vehicles. They averagedabout $1,500 profit on each car. Soon potential customers began tocome to them, asking for certain makes or models. If they found a good fit, they would buy it, service and detail it, then sell it.

They did this for about a year, and while it allowed them to stay afloat, Tom and Noemi realized that it was not going to be the right fit either. They would have to keep searching, keep trying, and keep hustling.

Once more on the Internet, Noemi discovered the subject of house flipping. She read up on the idea and showed her research to Tom. "Baby, we did such a wonderful job remodeling our cabin. How would you feel about buying houses, remodeling them, and then selling them for a profit?"

Tom answered slowly, "You know what? I tried that once, and it did not work out for me. I tried to buy foreclosures in the past, but I wanted a bank to finance them. Maybe we could do it a different way."

"How?"

"Well, we paid for a cabin already. Maybe we can borrow money against it and buy our houses."

Noemi was totally against the idea. Tom's credit score was improving, but she had no credit score of her own since she had no U.S. credit history. She felt borrowing against the cabin would mean they no longerowned it. Instead, it would belong to a mortgage company, and they would be further in debt.

But the more Tom considered the idea of house flipping, the more interested he became. With several days of convincing, he talked Noemi into exploring the idea. They went to a mortgage company, which first confirmed that Tom's credit score had increased to 620. Next, they appraised the cabin. Its value came back as $205,000. Tom and Noemi were stunned. What an improvement on their $55,000 investment! The mortgage company offered them a line of credit, and they quickly accepted.

They were in business.

10
Two of a Kind, Working on a Full House

Roswell, NM

Tom and Noemi stood in front of a foreclosed house in Roswell, NM, waiting for a real estate agent, about to take their biggest gamble yet. They had visited the town during mystery shopping visits but didn't know it well. And while they were both good at repair and remodel work, they couldn't be sure what they were about to see. But they were all in on this idea of flipping houses.

The realtor soon arrived and showed them around. The home had three bedrooms and two bathrooms, a beautiful fireplace, a covered patio, and a wooden fence in the back. The price was unbelievable, only $38,000. The inside was a little rough, but nothing they couldn't handle. Goober investigated the entire house, and he seemed to approve. That settled it. They let the realtor know that they planned to make an offer as soon as the finances were in order.

Their next stop was to the bank, where their friend Kurt introduced them to a tall, nice-looking woman named Robin. They had decided that instead of using their line of credit, they would try to get a mortgage on the property. Robin would be the woman to decide whether their dream would come true. And the first thing she did was sit down and run his credit score.

Sitting in her office, Tom held his breath as she searched. After a few minutes, she stated, "Not too bad. I think I can help you." Tom almost couldn't believe it—thanks to Noemi, his credit problems had disappeared.

Next, Robin drove with them to the property. She agreed that it was a great bargain. She pointed out a few problems: missing shingles on the roof, fence repairs, etc. Tom assured her, "This is what we do."

So, Robin took them back to her office, tapped on her computer for a while, and then announced, "I believe I can help you guys. I can loan you the amount you need on a one-year note, with interest due at the expiration of the note." Seeing their confusion, she smiled, "That means you will make no payments for a year, but at the end of the year, you will pay off the note with interest."

"How much interest are we talking about," Tom replied.

"$2,200."

"So, once a year has passed, we will owe you $40,200?"

"That's correct."

Tom and Noemi exchanged a look, and then he met the banker's eyes. "Okay, Robin, you got a deal."

As they pointed the truck back toward home, Noemi rolled down her window and shouted to the world, "We own two houses!" They had no idea where this adventure was going to lead them, but they knew they were going to do it together.

Taos County, NM

When they arrived back at the cabin, Noemi had another notice from the Naturalization Office. Her next appointment was in 10 days. The time between now and the house closing in Roswell was going to be busy.

They tried to use it wisely: going over the figures for remodeling the cabin to use as projections for this new project, planning the trip, paperwork for the new house, packing. They decided to take a mattress to the new house instead of paying for a hotel. Tom hadn't been sure how she would feel about staying in a run-down place, but Noemi just shrugged, "Hey, I did it here so that I can do it there."

They nervously set off for Albuquerque, and the appointment went smoothly. They re-did her fingerprints, told her that the process was now complete, and confirmed that she should receive her green card in the mail shortly. On the way home, Noemi bounced up and down, repeating, "I am legal. I have a green card. Now, I want to be an American citizen, and I want everyone to know that."

"Don't worry, they'll know," Tom laughed.

The next day, she announced, "Before we head to Roswell, I want to apply for Citizenship. I want to be an American." She went right to the computer to research the process. What she learned nearly broke her heart. "I must have my green card for three years before I can apply for citizenship," she cried.

"What? Why so long?"

"It says right here that once you receive a green card that a person cannot apply for citizenship for three years from that date. It seems they want you to be in this country for three years and not break any laws during that period before they will consider anyone for citizenship."

Tom gave her a comforting hug. "Write this date down so we will remember when three years have passed. I told you it would take time. Everything will be all right, they have rules, and we have to follow them. All we can do now is wait. Let's focus on Roswell squarely."

Noemi threw herself into preparations, and soon the cabin was a mess. Things for the trip laying everywhere—pots here, piles of sheets there, and stuff over there, and more stuff over there. Before they knew it, they were on the road. They looked like the Beverly Hillbillies, with a truck bed loaded to the brim and a mattress tied on top. It was a funny sight when they pulled up in front of the title company in Roswell. But even though Tom knew it looked ridiculous, he grabbed Noemi's hand and almost dragged her as he hurried inside to make the deal. It seemed like they signed 1,000 papers, but soon it was done. They hopped back in their Beverly Hillbilly truck with the key to their new home in hand.

Roswell, NM

They spent their first night in the "flip house" on the mattress in the middle of the floor with Goober's bed next to their bed. Then, the next morning, they made coffee and jumped right in. The kitchen needed new paint on the cabinets and walls, a new countertop, light fixtures, and tile. The bathrooms needed new toilets, vanities, light fixtures, tile, and paint. The bedrooms and the living room should have fresh paint, carpet, blinds, and light fixtures. There was a lot to do.

Noemi talked non-stop over breakfast at IHOP and rushed Tom through his meal so they could get to Home Depot. Silently, Tom worried about how they would pay for everything they needed. Their funds werelimited, and they shouldn't spend all they had on supplies. But theywere about to catch yet another lucky break.

On the way inside, Noemi saw an advertisement for Home Depot's credit card, which came with zero interest for a year. They went to the service department and applied. Within a few minutes, they were offered an account with a limit of $3,500. Tom frowned, "That's not enough." He explained to the clerk, "We flip houses for a living, and weneed to buy everything that's required." She agreed to let them talk to a supervisor at headquarters.

While the woman was on the phone, Noemi nudged Tom and grumbled, "Are you crazy? $3,500 is a lot of credit. We don't want them not to give us any credit at all."

Tom replied, "We'll see." A few minutes later, the clerk came back with good news saying; they could qualify for a business account with a $50,000 limit. Tom and Noemi were in shock. They found a bench nearby to collect their thoughts. After they sat down, Tom turned to Noemi, "Baby, do you realize that we can do this without spending any of our own money? We can buy the houses, and all the materials that weneed to remodel them with no out of the pocket expense." He leaned back on the bench, closed his eyes, and said with wonder, "Shit."

Noemi grabbed Tom's hand, pulled him up from the bench, and they began to shop. By the time they finished, they had seven carts full of tools; tiles; paint, brushes, and rollers; toilets; vanities; lights; and everything else on Noemi's list. She was having the time of her life. "This is so much fun!" she grinned.

At the checkout line, they got a lot of incredulous looks from other customers. When the cashier handed them their receipt for $7,652.35, she shook her head, saying, "Don't work too hard."

As he helped them load the truck, another employee asked, "Are you building a house?"

"Just remodeling," Tom laughed.

It was almost dark when they got back to the house, so they called it a day and went out for a bite to eat. During dinner, they discussed how God had been so good to them, watching over them and guiding them through everything they had done since they first met. Tom said, "It's asthough he will not let us make a mistake. If we try to do something andit is wrong, he always moves us in another direction until we finally endup doing the right thing. It's incredible."

Noemi agreed, "It's true; we are experiencing God's blessings."

For the next 30 days, Tom and Noemi worked harder than ever. She filled holes in walls, sanded, and painted. He gutted the bathrooms and installed new fixtures, laid tile, and grouted for hours. Whenever they met in the hallway, they would stop for a hug and a kiss. Sometimes Noemi would sneak up behind Tom to kiss his neck. He would grin mischievously, "Careful. Don't start something you can't finish."

They watered the neglected lawn and cleared the yard of tree limbs and weeds, painted in the heat of the desert summer. They installed a light fixture towel rack, dragged old toilets outside, and cut lumber. They brought in a plumber to help connect the new fixtures. Tom built a beautiful new redwood countertop for the kitchen.

It was hard work, especially for two people over age 50. Tom began to experience crippling pain. During his Vietnam days as a machine gunner, he had carried a forty-pound machine gun, twenty pounds of ammo, and a sixty-pound backpack everywhere he went. Now, he was discovering the long-term toll of that load. Several times, a disc in Tom's back would slip out of place, and he would be bedridden. Noemi would apply a heating pad and massage the muscles with an electric vibrator.

At last, after a month, the work came to an end. They walked from room to room, admiring their handy work.

"Baby, that countertop is beautiful!"

"These colors are amazing! I had no idea you could paint so well."

Noemi would squeal with delight, and every time, Goober would run back and forth through the rooms. She looked at Tom with shining eyes and said, "Who would not want to buy this house?"

It was time to sell.

Next, Tom and Noemi learned several important lessons about realestate. At first, they thought part of the fun would be selling it themselves. Why pay 6% to a realtor for something you could do? They bought "for sale by owner" signs and put them in the yard, and placedan ad in the newspaper. After a few days of little response, they held an open house. It seemed to be a tremendous success, with lots of potential buyers stopping in to look, but no offers made yet. It was as if thebuyers would show up, then leave, never to be heard from again. Asthey learned more about the city, the couple understood the economy of the city had been facing depression for the past fifty years, because the air force base had closed. The buyers must be out there somewhere. They brought in a professional realtor.

Since there was nothing else they could do with the house but wait, they found another foreclosed house. The price for this one was $20,000. They went back to Robin, quickly closed the deal, and found themselves in the middle of the floor in another run-down house. Another 30 days and they had another house ready to go. But once again, they seemed to have no luck selling it.

Perhaps they needed to go home and regroup.

Taos County, NM

Goober was thrilled to be back home. He had accepted that in the city, he was limited to the back yard and the leash. He enjoyed going for walks in the neighborhood. But his true love was the mountains, where he was free to roam.

They spent a quiet weekend at the cabin, and Tom put together a new plan. He wrote a fact sheet for each house, complete with a photo. At the bottom of each, he printed: "If you need help with financing, we can help." The way he saw it, they had good contacts with Kurt, Robin, and other mortgage brokers. If a potential buyer was interested in a house, Tom and Noemi could check their credit, then take them to the appropriate lender. Armed with all this new knowledge, Tom, Noemi and Goober drove back to Roswell.

Roswell, NM

They arrived on Friday, so they stopped by the newspaper office to buy an "Open House" ad. They decided to run the ad for a week and have an open house every day until they found a buyer. They both understood that it was vital to sell the houses, as both had banknotes against them. Plus, the couple owed Home Depot more than $15,000. These houses had to sell, and soon.

To their surprise, House #1 was full of potential buyers on the first Saturday, and everyone was interested in Tom's offer to help with financing. However, a father and daughter came in who already had their financing. The father signed the contract on that day.

The Bradburn's breathed a sigh of relief. This sale would pay off the house and the Home Depot balance. "Now we are rolling," said Noemi.

"It seems that way. Let's get the other house sold. Then I will agree with you completely."

They used the same technique on House #2. And to their joy, they got the same results. They signed a contract on the first open house day. With that sale, they paid off the loan and banked twenty-eight thousand dollars. They were dumbfounded. Without spending a cent of their own money, and in sixty days, they pocketed fifty thousand dollars. They headed back to the cabin for a well-deserved week off.

11
Turn, Turn, Turn

The Bradburn's developed a rhythm for their house-flipping, and before they knew it, three years passed.

Those three years were busy years with several challenges. They had traveled constantly between Taos County, Albuquerque, and Roswell.

Some houses presented more challenges than others did. One was beautiful and only $20,000 to buy, but Noemi felt nervous and unsafe in the neighborhood. She was thankful to have Goober with them. Another just had a strange, spooky feeling, and they both breathed a sigh of relief when it sold. Other houses had different problems: needing a new roof, or a new a/c, and so on. No matter what they faced, Tom and Noemi were having the time of their lives. They even developed a following of people who would stop by their open houses to check out Tom and Noemi's latest gem.

Facilitating the financing process seemed to work like magic. They learned that many people were afraid to go to a mortgage company alone, and liked having someone to introduce them to a lender. It gave Tom and Noemi an advantage, too, by allowing them to monitor the progress of a loan. In a few cases, they even covered a buyer's down payment, carrying it as a second mortgage to help facilitate a sale.House flipping became a terrific business, one that they both loved and cherished.

There were unexpected difficulties and setbacks, and they occasionally had to look for creative solutions. In one situation, a couple for whom they had covered the down payment began experiencing financial trouble. The couple stopped paying both their mortgage and the debt they owed Tom and Noemi and were very close to foreclosure and bankruptcy. In the end, they offered to buy back the house. Tom negotiated an agreement for the couple to receive $2000 cash to start over. The Bradburn's resumed ownership of the property, gave it a quick clean up, and sold it a second time for another $18,000 profit.

There were personal challenges to meet, as well. Tom continued to experience anxiety attacks at least once a month, where his breathing would become labored, his heart would beat out of control, and he felt as though he might jump out of his skin. Sometimes he would wake up in the middle of the night in a cold sweat and would have to get out of bed and pace for hours to calm himself down. He also suffered occasional bouts of anger, which seemed to happen for no reason at all. Out of the blue, he would feel mad or irritable, and the feelings would last for several hours and then go away. Noemi learned that arguingwith Tom during these angry moments only made the situation worse. Her only option was to keep her mouth shut and wait. These anxiety andanger attacks puzzled both Tom and Noemi, and all they could do was live with them, their families too experienced growth and change. Lauraand Pablo had a second daughter. Jeff and his partner Kris had a baby boy. While he and Tom still struggled with communication, Jeff did invite the Bradburn's to meet their grandson. Tom and Noemi spent a few days in Massachusetts. Unfortunately, Jeff went back to radio silence after this visit. Eric, feeling that his life had gotten off track, decided the Army might give him some structure and stability. Tom was proud of his younger son but also worried. He was still suffering the aftereffects of his own experiences in Vietnam, and he knew wars were ongoing in both Afghanistan and Iraq. He could only hope Eric would stay safe. They traveled to Georgia to watch his son's Army graduation ceremony, and Tom thought back to his Marine boot camp graduation. They had a couple of days with Eric before he moved to his base in NewYork, and they drove back to Roswell.

After seven houses, Tom and Noemi began taking a cruise after each flip. They traveled to the Bahamas, Hawaii, and other beautiful places. After their fourteenth house, they met Brian and Dara, a couple ofpotential buyers who became good friends and played poker with them often. This couple loved visiting a small beach town in Ecuador called Bahia de Caraquez, and they often tried to convince Tom and Noemi to come down there and see them. But the house flipping business kept them too busy for planning long vacations (aside from their celebratory cruises, of course), and Noemi was busy with her citizenship process.

Albuquerque, NM

Noemi's last naturalization appointment required a citizenship quiz. The office gave her a list of one hundred questions, and she frantically studied for the test like a grade-schooler for a final exam. She was excited but nervous. All she wanted was for it to be over. The night before the test, she could not sleep. She stayed up studying until she passed out with her head resting on the kitchen table.

When they called her number, Tom watched Noemi disappear into the next room. To his surprise, he waited less than 10 minutes before she came out again. He thought something terrible had happened, but then he saw she was almost floating across the floor. He stood. "What happened?"

Noemi could barely speak, "I passed the test."

"So quickly?"

"Yes, it was an oral test, and they only asked five questions. First, they asked who the President of the United States is? The second was, how many stars does the American flag have? Then, how long is the term of the President of the United States, and what was the name of the ship that brought Christopher Columbus to discover America? And finally, how often does the United States have the Presidential elections?"

Tom shook his head. "Only five questions? All that studying for five little questions?"

"Yes. And we will have to attend the swearing-in ceremony next week."

"Wow. So quickly. A person waits and waits and waits, and then, suddenly, it's done."

The following week, Tom and Noemi drove from Roswell to Santa Fe, New Mexico, for Noemi's citizenship ceremony. To Noemi, it was one of the most special days of her life. They swore she and about fifty others in, and she cried through most of it. In the end, when they played "America the Beautiful," she broke down once again. Finally, they called everyone upfront, one by one, to receive their citizenship certificate, and then it was over. Tom's beautiful wife was an American citizen. It took five long years and a lot of ups and downs, but they finally did it.

Taos County, NM

One day, out of the blue, the phone rang. It was Eric, who said, "Dad, I'm leaving for Afghanistan next week."

"Oh son," gasped Tom, "I can't believe it. I was hoping that you might miss the action over there."

"Nope."

"Son, listen to these words and listen carefully. Keep your head down, your eyes open, and stay focused every day."

"Dad, don't worry. I have a lot of things to do with this life of mine, and I will survive this. I will be around a lot of good men. They'll watch my back."

"I'm still going to worry. I will think about you every day. I love you, Son."

"I love you, too, Dad."

The year passed very slowly, and Tom watched the news every day to see if he could hear any news about Eric's unit. Fortunately, there was nothing. At last, they scheduled Eric's unit to come home. Tom and Noemi flew to New York, where they met up with Eric's mom, as well as Jeff, Kris, and their son Cian. There they joined many other families in a crowded gym to wait for the returning soldiers. When they spotted Eric, they rushed forward, and Tom and Eric fell into each other's arms as only a father and son could. Tears of happiness flowed everywhere in the gym.

Soon after, Eric received an honorable discharge, and he moved to Texas to be close to his mother. Later, he met a woman named Rachel. They had Tom's second grandson, Ryan, together and moved to Denver, CO. Tom was glad they were only a 5-hour drive away.

Roswell, NM

Eventually, Tom and Noemi approached the age of sixty, and they realized it was time to slow down. By this time, they had successfully flipped over twenty houses, eight in the last year alone. They seemed financially on top of the world. Their credit scores had jumped to more than 800 points each, their borrowing power had reached an incredible level, and they had funded over 10 wonderful cruises all over the world.

They had made some unusual deals. During their twenty-first sale, the buyers, an older couple, did not want to put up any earnest money. The gentleman, a preacher, explained: "I believe in faith and people's word, not in financial restraints." He then had them join hands in a circle and prayed for a good outcome with their purchase of the home. Tom and Noemi had never been involved in a situation like this one before. They both thought that earnest money was a universally accepted first step in purchasing a house; they were suspicious but agreed to go along and take the house off the market while they waited for the closing. It was a long, nerve-wracking month, but the closing went off without a hitch.

Not everything was sunshine, however. Noemi had started to feel ill. She began to experience terrible pain in her rectum and anus and difficulties using the bathroom. Instead of going away, it was getting steadily worse over time. It got in the way of several parts of the couple's life, especially their intimacy. And her doctor could not figure out what was wrong.

Then disaster struck. It was the year 2008, and the housing economy collapsed. People across the country stopped buying homes. In Roswell, already no stranger to economic depression, the market dried up.

At the time, Tom and Noemi had five unsold homes. They could not even find anyone to look at one of their houses. For weeks, they anxiously discussed what to do. At last, Tom said, "We don't have a choice. We will have to rent these houses and wait to see what happens with the economy."

"But we have banknotes due to three of them."

"We'll have to get mortgages. The renters will make the monthly payments."

As it turned out, mortgage money was difficult to come by. The rules had become so confining that only the strongest of customers could get a loan. Fortunately for Tom and Noemi, they were in the small group who were able to qualify. They took mortgages out on three of their four properties and found renters. The fourth house they sold on a contract because that had become the only way anyone, with shaky credit or borderline income, could purchase a home. For the fifth, they also found tenants. But their New Mexico house flipping business, for the foreseeable future, was at an end.

They would have to find a new way forward.

12
Ocean Front Property

Taos County, NM

With their house flipping business at an end, Tom and Noemi relied on their rental properties for their income. Tom reached the retirement age of 62 and applied for social security, but after the recent downturn, they worried the government might run out of money to fund the program. So, they weren't sure how long they would receive his monthly $1,200 check. Now, it seemed great credit scores and financial strength hadlittle influence. They were facing a drastic change in their circumstances.

One day, Tom asked Noemi, "Do you remember when Brian and Dara told us about Ecuador?"

"Yes. He kept saying how cheap it was to live there. Beachfront condos for $25,000. Great meals for three or four dollars each."

"Maybe we should look into that city of Bahia de Caraquez."

So, Noemi got down to her research. Bahia de Caraquez, Ecuador, started to look like a magical place. They decided a trip down there was in order.

The priority was to get passports for both of them first. Tom explained how they would go to the post office to get them.

"The post office?" Noemi asked, baffled.

Tom explained the process, and she shook her head in wonder. "I love this country. Everything is so simple." They drove into Taos, had their pictures taken, and filled out the paperwork. Ten days later received their passports in the mail.

Looking at hers, Noemi gushed, "Now I feel like a true American. I have my American passport."

Tom shrugged. "I have never looked at you as anything other than American." She gave him a big hug.

Travel planning went smoothly, though they were surprised how complicated it was to get to Bahia. They would have to fly to Dallas, then to Miami, then to Quito, Ecuador, and finally to Manta, Ecuador. There they would take a two-hour taxi ride to the little beach community. Goober would have to board at the vet's office in New Mexico. They hoped a 12-day trip would be enough to decide whether this was the right move.

Bahia de Caraquez, Ecuador

The roads were all dirt and treacherous to travel on, but finally, they made it to their hotel by the ocean. It was too late to see much of the town, but Noemi opened the sliding glass doors. She sighed, "Oh, Baby, this is incredible. Listen to the waves. This takes my breath away."

They slept like babies after their long trip and woke to a beautiful view outside. They took in the sun and the sound of the waves for a few minutes, and then went down to breakfast. There, Tom realized he might have some challenges in Ecuador. He spoke not a word of Spanish, and no one there spoke English. To order at the restaurant, he had to tell Noemi what he wanted and have her translate.

But their walk after breakfast showed how charming the town was. The beach was incredibly wide and long and empty. Like a child, Noemi kicked her shoes off and began running toward the water. After a moment, Tom joined her. They walked hand in hand in the sand. She pointed across the bay and asked, "I wonder how people get to that other city." Soon, they came upon an area where small boats were coming and going. After watching for a moment, they asked someone who explained that these were small water taxis that carried people across the bay. They paid their fifteen cents, the ferry fee across the water. Noemi enjoyed the feel of the wind and the spray as they traveled.

On the opposite shore, they looked around in surprise. "What a small town," Noemi said.

"It did look larger from the other side," agreed Tom.

Noemi stopped a number of the locals to ask questions. She soon found out that there were several fishing villages close by, and bigger towns a few miles away. They agreed to come back and explore them another day and then took a water taxi back to Bahia.

Safely back, they realized that they had walked the entire distancearound the peninsula, which was about two miles. Around them, bicycles zipped by, each one towing a covered bench. These were bicycle taxis. This was a novelty they could not resist. They flagged onedown and asked for a tour of the town.

It turned out there was not much to see. Within twenty minutes, and for the price of fifty cents, they had toured the whole place. They had discovered the open market, several little tiendas, convenience stores, hardware stores, and places for household goods. There were no big grocery stores, malls, or shopping centers. "Where do people shop for food?" She asked the taxi cyclist.

"In Manta."

"Wow. Manta is two hours from here!" Noemi exclaimed. The cyclist shrugged.

Back at the hotel, Noemi asked Tom, "Don't you love this place?"

"Sure, but where would we get groceries, furniture, and stuff?"

"Ha! Details. Let's go down to the lobby and ask."

Tom stood outside for a smoke as Noemi talked to the desk clerk and other locals. Everything seemed totally upside down from what he knew; he could not deny the place was magical. When he went back inside, Noemi was ready to share what she had learned: "In Manta, they have real malls and supermarkets and anything else a person may need."

"Yeah, but that is two hours away."

"Yes, but at the cabin, the shopping is thirty-five minutes away, and we survive."

"Thirty-five minutes is not two hours."

"Baby, we could go for supplies every two weeks or once a month. Sometimes it might be good to get away and do some shopping or watch a movie."

Tom was running out of objections, so he asked: "Okay, now what?"

"I think we should look at condos."

They decided to go back to the method they knew best, which is knocking at the doors of each apartment and asking if it had units for sale. Each building had a guardian in charge of them.

The couple checked other places and found out that either the condo was a mess, too large, too small, or too expensive. Finally, on their twelfth try, they found a very nice little apartment building tucked away behind another building. A place was available on the seventh floor. It smelled a bit musty, but the guardian assured them that it was because they had closed the house for a few months now. There were three bedrooms and two baths, plus a tiny, simple suite intended as servant's quarters. While the neighboring building partially blocked the ocean view, it still had lovely views of the town.

As veteran remodelers, Tom and Noemi had a vision and saw how this place could fill their needs. "How much are the owners asking?" Noemi said.

The guardian answered, "$62,000 American."

"Seems a little high to me," Noemi replied, "Who would I talk to about the price?"

"I'll call the owners tonight and see what they have to say."

"Then we'll be back tomorrow," Noemi agreed.

As they left the building, Tom turned to Noemi, "Where are the $25,000 condos that Brian promised us?"

"I don't know, but do you realize that one of these would cost four or five million in California"?

"That's true, but in California, we would have a mall and supermarket."

Noemi just laughed.

The next morning, they returned, and the guardian let them know that the best price the owner was willing to take was $54,000. Noemi said, "Wow, that's a good deal!"

"Yeah, but it's not $25,000," Tom grumbled.

Noemi replied, "Don't care. It's still a good deal for a beachfront property."

"It's not exactly beachfront. We have a big building between us and the beach."

"Baby, it's a good deal!"

"Let's go home to the cabin and figure it out."

Taos County, NM

When they got back, the couple went for a walk to talk things over. Noemi said, "Baby, most of our cash is tied up in houses. We're about

$15,000 short of what we need to buy the condo. What are we going to do?"

As usual, the Lord stepped in. Out of the clear blue sky, a friend of theirs called and wanted to increase his available rental properties, but couldn't get a loan to buy any more. He wondered if they would sell him one of theirs. The couple had one house, in particular, that was a good fit for his needs. Tom told him that if he would assume the mortgage payments on the house, and pay them $24,000 in cash, then they would sell it to him. This gave them the funds they needed to buy the Bahia condo. They took a leap of faith and made the deal.

Tom and Noemi decided that they would spend the winter months on the beach and the summer months in the mountains. But they had one serious concern: Goober. Ecuador had a ban on purebred pit bulls. So, Noemi did the research and figured out that if they could get a veterinarian to certify that Goober was a mixed breed, they should be able to take him. They got his records in order, and the veterinarian typed the letter of confirmation for them. They soon learned that an animal could not travel on any plane unless the animal could travel in a temperature-controlled area, or if the outside temperature at the time of the flight was above eighty-six degrees. They were going to have to buy him a crate of the proper size, too. Continental Airlines was the only company currently offering temperature-controlled areas for pets.

Because they did not want Goober to have to change planes in Dallas, and then Miami, in Quito, and finally to Manta—as they had done— they found a direct flight from Galveston, Tx to Quito. This flight was very expensive, but there was no other choice. They bought the tickets, and a new crate then rented an SUV and drove the 15 hours to Galveston.

Once they arrived at the airport, they spent a chaotic period loading Goober in the cage. Once that was done, tears began to flow from their eyes as they assured Goober that everything would be okay before they shuttled him out of their sight.

Mariscal Sucre Airport, Ecuador

The flight to Quito seemed long, and they worried about their pet's well-being. Worse, when they landed, Tom and Noemi expected to see Goober in the baggage claim area, but he was not there. In a panic, they asked an employee, and they gave them directions to a warehouse on the airport property. It was about twenty blocks away.

They made the trek with five or six bags in tow, through breathtaking heat. After asking directions from several airport employees, they finally found the warehouse. At the very back of the large, dark building, in the very corner, with several other cages and boxes on top of his cage, the couple found Goober.

Noemi found an employee and asked, "Can I take my dog to pee?"

"No ma'am, that is a Pitbull, and you cannot take it out of its cage."

She tried to show him the paperwork from the vet, but the man could not read English. Finally, Noemi lost her temper. She began to scream at the man in Spanish. At last, he gave up and agreed they could walk their dog. They put on his leash and took him outside, then gave him some water. He quickly drank it all down.

Next, Tom and Noemi learned that they were not allowed to move Goober from the building without the proper paperwork. Noemi asked, "What the heck are you talking about, what paperwork?" Noemi was required to go to eight or nine different places to grease everyone's palms. Tom waited with the bags and Goober.

After a couple of hours, Noemi, hot and worn out, returned. The paperwork authorized the employees to load Goober onto the plane they would take to Manta. Once again, Tom and Noemi cried when they took Goober away.

Finally, they were all reunited in Manta, Ecuador. Goober seemed extremely disoriented, stressed, and tired, but his tail was wagging nonetheless. It was after 10 at night, in Manta, and they struggled to find a taxi driver willing to take the 2-hour trip to Bahia. All the drivers were worried about thieves and robbers on the road. At last, the trio found someone willing to take them all and loaded Goober and the bags into the SUV.

The taxi driver started, and soon Tom and Noemi realized it was not a route that they were familiar with. Remembering what other drivers had said, she began to worry that they were about to be kidnapped. "Where are you going?" She asked. He assured her that the roads in the other direction were under construction as the government was building a new highway system, and this was the only way. Tom and Noemi put their faith in God; they gritted their teeth and talked to Goober during the trip.

Bahia de Caraquez, Ecuador

Finally, they arrived in front of the apartment building, all worn out. Goober, the happiest camper of the three, was just glad to have the trip behind him and to have his feet on the solid ground finally. He was thrilled to have Tom walk him to a park across the street. He was less thrilled about the elevator ride up to the condo. He lay on the floor and whimpered as it traveled upward.

Upstairs, Tom took Goober out on the balcony to see the view. Goober took one look through the railing, and he backed up in fear. It would be days before the dog would approach the railing, though he eventually fell in love with the balcony.

They soon adjusted to life in the little beach town. Tom would say that Goober went from being a mountain dog to being a balcony dog. He even got used to the elevator, since it represented a walk. He didn't get along with the stray dogs in the area, though. Things would start well enough, with the two dogs touching noses and sniffing rear ends. But then Goober would plant his front legs firmly and stand up straight and strong as if to say, "I am the boss of this area." Then, the other dog would growl, "I don't think so," and inevitably start a fight. They could tell their dog missed the mountains, but never took him on their trips back to the cabin. The first plane trip had been too stressful for them all.

Noemi soon found herself in conflict, too. After talking to the guardian several times, she discovered that the building administrator was not paying bills on behalf of the building. The guardian had not been paid in a couple of months, either. The administrator was pocketing the money.

Noemi began gathering evidence to support this claim. Eventually, when she had her case built, she called a meeting of the condo owners. She showed them what they had discovered; the group fired their administrator and hired her to take his place. This new job carried a generous salary of $300 per month.

This led to other discoveries, such as the fact that the building had no city water. Instead, it was trucked into the building several times per week; it seems as though the mayor of the city owned all of the water trucks, and he had no interest in repairing the city water pipes. Nevertheless, Noemi began the arduous task of collecting expense money from the condo owners. Each one owed a monthly fee for costs like electricity, water, guardian salary, taxes, swimming pool maintenance, and periodic building repairs. She got them all on track, and soon the money began to flow. She got all of the payments up to date and began to make beautiful improvements such as paint, landscaping, and stone facades for the ugly parts of the walls. Shebecame a hero to the other condo owners.

Walking Goober in the morning, Noemi would say, "Baby, I think I'm going to love this place. It's so beautiful and peaceful."

Tom would agree, "It's certainly different than any life that I have known."

Of course, they soon began their usual round of renovations. They built the condos with blocks and plaster, unfamiliar materials that made remodeling a nervous proposition for Tom. They decided to hire professionals for this project. They had new kitchen cabinets and a large "L" shaped bar hand-built in wood with a dark cherry color. They installed new granite countertops. They also had new wooden closets built for the bedrooms and brought in two men to paint the whole place. Then they ordered new furniture, especially a new bed, as Tom could not get used to the one that had come with the place.

The whole process took six months, and when it was over, they made an uncomfortable discovery. The city was boring. They had explored it fully in no time at all. There were a few restaurants, no places to shop, no movies, and not many gringos. While the beauty was there, that is allthere was.

Noemi soon read about a city called Salinas, which was a little larger, and also on the coast. They got together a group of friends to take a bus trip there. All five of them fell in love with Salinas, especially an area called Chipipe, which had a huge, beautiful beach. The high-rise condo buildings were beautiful, and it felt less commercial than the mainSalinas beach.

Salinas seemed to have everything Tom and Noemi were looking for. It was larger, and it had modern and up-to-date supermarkets. It also had a mall with a movie theater and popcorn, which made Tom happy. They decided this was the city for them.

In Bahia, since they had made up their minds to move, they put their condo up for sale. They had a banner made and hung it over their rail. Noemi started her usual campaign of research and found several condos in Salinas within their price range. She talked to real estate agents and made appointments. They made a solo trip to Salinas to check them out.

The trip started with the best possible omen. As soon as they had arrived in the city, Noemi got a call on her cell. One of their neighbors in the condo building wanted to talk about buying their unit. He wasn't bothered by the price, and Tom and Noemi were hopeful.

Unfortunately, when the first agent they met showed them several places, Tom and Noemi were not crazy about what they saw. Yet, they wanted so much to live in this town. One place, a fifth-floor unit on the main street, seemed ok. It needed a lot of work and remodeling, but the price was low, and they knew they had the know-how to whip the place into shape. Noemi still wasn't sure. "It seems to be very loud in this area. Don't you remember last night when the disco got cranked up, and we weren't able to sleep? I think it will be like that every night in this neighborhood."

"I'm not crazy about it either, but of all the units that we have seen, this one seems to be our last choice."

The next morning, they reluctantly made an offer. When the agent contacted the owner, she said she would think about it and call back.

While they waited to hear, Tom and Noemi decided to visit another agent. They explained their dilemma to him, especially the part about making an offer on a unit they did not love. He replied, "Before you buy any condo, I have one that I want to show you."

They got in his car, and to their surprise, he drove them straight to Chipipe. Noemi protested, "This must be a mistake. We cannot afford a place here."

He laughed, "Based on the information you have given me, I believe you can."

As they drove, Tom compared the two neighborhoods in his head. The other one was rundown and full of open restaurants, tiendas, and those dang loud discos. This one was quite well kept up, quiet, and totally without discos, restaurants, or any commercial activities.

The agent stopped at the smallest building in the neighborhood. The maintenance wasn't quite as good as the others. Noemi had doubts about what they were about to see. Then, on the eleventh floor, the agent unlocked the door and swung it open. The beauty of the place took Noemi's breath away. She could not believe the difference in this condo and all the others they had seen. It was perfect, needing no remodeling. It was bright, with a nautical theme. It also had some very high-end furniture and was decorated exceptionally well. The walls were painted bright white with a splash of blue here and there. The pictures on the walls had blue frames, the lamps had blue shades, and the leather sofa was a deep blue. Walking through the three bedrooms and two baths, she said, "It's a dream. This is a joke, right?"

The agent protested, "No joke!" They all stood together at the rail of the living room, looking down on the beautiful Chipipe beach. It was a million-dollar view. Finally, the agent asked them to have a seat and talk about the price.

Noemi started. "I saw this unit online. One website said the price was $98,000. Another said, $90,000. So, what is the real price?"

He explained, "The owner changed agents, and once they gave me the listing, they also dropped the price to $90,000."

"I told you that we could not pay anything like $90,000."

"I know. Noemi, I think you could offer $80,000, and the sellers would accept. You see, the owner's son lives in Florida. The sellers are desperate to move so they can be closer to him."

"Well, we can offer $75,000 now and $5,000 in three months. Today we're a little tight on cash, and it would be better for us to go that way."

"I'll see what they say."

Tom and Noemi walked over to the railing as the agent made his call. Staring at the view, Noemi said, "This is breathtaking, huh, Baby?"

"This can't be. This is the most unbelievable condo I have ever seen, and this million-dollar view is to kill for." They looked down at the rows of tents and umbrellas on the beach. The people in the water seemed so small. Everything was quiet and peaceful.

Then the agent stepped up to them. He was smiling. "They accepted your offer."

Noemi began to cry. She stretched her arms out, as if welcoming a relative, and shouted, "This is ours! Can it be true? This lovely place is ours!"

They went back to Bahia while waiting for the deal to close, and to finalize the sale of their current place. Fortunately, the couple loved the Bahia place, and they made a deal instantly. After they left, Noemi hugged Tom, saying, "You see, the Lord continues to work in ourlives."

"Yep. That is the only way to explain this. It was the Lord's doing."

After that, everything seemed to fall into place. Both deals closed quickly. The son of the Bahia guardian had a truck and offered to move their things to Salinas. Noemi pointed towards the sky and said, "God, once again."

Salinas, Ecuador

The difference in Bahia and Chipipe was like the difference in night and day. The Chipipe condo was directly overlooking the beach, with no building blocking their view. Goober had no trouble adjusting to the new place and made himself right at home. There were fewer stray dogs in the area, which made walks more relaxing for Tom, and Goober was also happy since he had all new territory to mark. Life was good.

Noemi had stayed on as administrator of the Bahia condo association. Then, early on the second morning in their new place in Chipipe, she noticed a water truck pulling into the building. She went straight to the guardian to find out what was going on.

Once again, she heard from a building guardian the administrator was not dealing honestly with; he had not been paying the water bill, so the city had turned off the water, and now they had to truck water in. Healso described how the administrator owed everyone money, and paid none of the three guardians on staff in two months. She put a hand onher head and groaned, "No. Not again."

Once again, Noemi began to play detective. She gathered evidence. She went to the city offices to check their records, where she discovered that the building owed more than $20,000 to the city for taxes, as well as to the guardians, the elevator repairman, and other maintenance people. Once again, she called an emergency meeting with the condo owners and presented her evidence. The group immediately fired the current administrator and hired Noemi to straighten out the mess. Now she had two jobs.

She got straight to work, making deals with everyone owed money by the condo owners. She collected funds from their fellow residents, many of whom were months behind. Some owed $2000-3000, and one even owed $7000. It took a monumental effort to repair the damage done by the last administration, but within a year, they paid all of the vendorsand all the owners were current on their building fees. Once again, Noemi triumphed.

13
The Big D

Salinas, Ecuador

In addition to her work as an administrator for two condo buildings, Noemi had been holding down another position since the closure of their house flipping business: family accountant. Tom had always controlled his finances before, both as during his previous marriages and as a single father. But he was willing to let Noemi handle their money.

This steadily grew into a source of conflict between them, however. When he wanted cash, he would have to go to his wife and ask for it. There were times when he would say, "I need some money," and she would reply, "Baby, I just gave you twenty dollars two days ago. What did you do with it?" Tom began to feel that he had to justify everypenny he spent, where he spent it, and why he spent it.

Soon, there were daily arguments about money. Eventually, these led to arguments about anything and everything. Tom might say, "It's a beautiful sunny day, and there is not a cloud in the sky," and Noemi would respond, "There are a lot of clouds in the sky, and it's not sunnyat all." Then the day would be lost to fighting about the sky.

There came a day that a big fight broke out, and Tom blurted out, "When we get back to the States, I want a divorce!"

Noemi sighed, "That's fine. I am tired of living like this."

They did not discuss it further during their time in Salinas, but Tom did not forget.

Taos County, NM

True to his word, when they returned to the cabin, Tom announced, "I'm still going to file for a divorce."

Noemi was taken back because they had not discussed the idea since the argument in Ecuador. But she tried to stay calm. "Okay, but can we wait until next Wednesday to file?"

"Why next Wednesday?"

"Because next Wednesday will be our tenth anniversary, and I will be eligible for half of your social security."

Tom agreed.

The following Thursday, Tom filed the papers with the court. They had reached a mutual agreement concerning the division of property: Noemi would get the cabin, the condo in Ecuador, two of the Roswell properties, and eight thousand dollars in cash. Tom would get one rentalproperty that they owned outright, and two more that were still under mortgage, the car, some of the furniture from the cabin, and eightthousand dollars in cash. Because they had settled things amiably, the schedule of a court date was quick.

Sooner than either one wanted the date arrived. They both showed up to stand before the judge. From the bench, he said, "I have your decree in front of me, and it seems that there is mutual agreement on all settlements. Is that correct?"

Both Tom and Noemi responded, "Yes, your honor."

"Then, the case is now closed." And just like that, Tom and Noemi were divorced.

Even after this, the couple spent the rest of the summer together. Noemi helped Tom move his belongings to a storage unit in Las Vegas, New Mexico. When the day came for Noemi to return to Ecuador, Tom drove her to the airport. They both cried as she walked through security.

As her plane took off, Noemi lamented to herself, "I love that man, and I don't know what I am going to do without him."

Tom stood in front of the large window facing the airstrip. He felt his heart sink as he watched the plane rise in the sky. Then he pointed the truck toward Denton, where he hoped to find a place to live. He drove for ten straight hours before checking into a hotel room. The nextmorning, he bought a newspaper and began searching for an apartment. He wound up renting a place right across the street from the hotel. "It's not the greatest," he told himself, "But it is clean, close to restaurants, a supermarket, and the mall." He signed a one-year lease with the idea of starting a new life.

Salinas, Ecuador/Denton, TX, USA

Noemi spent the fall in her lonely condo. She went out with her Chipipe friends now and then, but told no one about the divorce. She was too embarrassed. So, if someone asked, she would only say that Tom was in the U.S. taking care of some business.

Tom was sad and lonely, too, having no work, and no friends. He played golf alone. Eric stopped by occasionally, especially on Dallas Cowboys Day, but he was busy with his own life. Tom tried buying a new home, a duplex where he thought he might live on one side and rent out the other. But after a long mortgage application process that was made difficult by the divorce, the property owner died, and the deal sank like a lead balloon. Weeks and months seem to crawl by.

Then, Tom and Noemi began to chat online once again, just like old times. They would meet up at 7 p.m. Tom's time. Sometimes they would skip a few days when Noemi was traveling for her buildingadministrator job in Bahia, but they'd pick up again when she returnedto Chipipe. Sometimes she would send word that her Internet was down,especially in Bahia, and they wouldn't chat for days. Tom worried aboutthis, but he remembered what life was sometimes like there.

This went on for a couple of weeks. Then, suddenly, their chats stopped altogether. Noemi was not online. Nor did she e-mail. Tom could not understand what had happened. Then, one day, he got an e-mail from her.

Hello Tom,

I have not been on messenger for the past few days because while in Bahia, I met someone. We went to dinner a few times and spent almost every day together for the past couple of weeks. I thought you might be wondering, so I decided that I needed to write to you and let you know what is going on. My time with this man has been short, but I think that you and I will never reconcile, so I began to spend time with him. His name is Bob, and he is a very good man. I think he is the man for me, and I just wanted to let you know so that you do not sit around your apartment waiting to hear from me again. I don't know what else to say. So, I will say goodbye.

Tom read the e-mail again and again. It broke his heart, but he realized that all of this was his fault. He deserved this. He wrote a reply stating that he was very happy for her (this, of course, was a lie) and that he loved her (which was true). Then he explained that it would be best if they did not communicate in the future.

Twenty minutes later, his phone rang. Noemi's voice, tearful and shaking, was on the other end of the line. "I don't love this man," she cried, "I am sorry I told you I did. Ever since I met him, I've been nervous and having anxiety attacks. I don't know why I sent you that email. I love you. I could never love anyone else."

For the first time in months, Tom felt happy and hopeful. "Then send him an e-mail saying that the two of you are done with and that we're getting back together."

Noemi sent the e-mail right away and sent a copy to Tom. She even forwarded the man's response, telling her goodbye.

Tom wasted no time. He sold his furniture, bought a ticket for Guayaquil, and was soon back home in Chipipe, in the arms of the love of his life, where he belonged.

14
The Big C

Buenos Aires, Argentina

Noemi was on a plane to visit Pablo. She and Tom had decided it was best he stayed in Chipipe with Goober this time, so she was on her own. She had struck up a conversation with the man in the seat next to her.

"I'm a Vietnam veteran," he told her, "And I am on disability forPTSD." He talked to her at length about his experience of the war.

"PDTS? PSTD? What is that?" Noemi asked.

He laughed, "PTSD. It stands for Post-Traumatic Stress Disorder."

"My husband, Tom, is also a Vietnam Veteran. He was a Marine machine gunner there."

"You need to tell him to apply for disability. If he was in Vietnam and he was a machine gunner, then I know that he has PTSD," the man said gravely.

"How would I know?"

"Let me ask you, does your husband have anxiety problems?"

"Yes."

"Does he have problems sleeping?"

"Yes."

"Anger issues?"

Noemi nodded, "Absolutely. A lot of anxiety and a lot of anger. He also has terrible back problems."

"Then, he has PTSD, and you need to get him help."

Noemi thought about this for the rest of the flight. She would much rather think about helping Tom than her problem. Before leaving for Buenos Aires, she had admitted to Tom that she wanted to see her old doctor as well as her son. Her pain and discomfort had gotten steadily worse, and they still could not figure out what was wrong. She hopedher longtime family doctor could help.

When Pablo picked her up from the airport, she tried to avoid the topic at first. She asked about his work, and his girlfriend, Laura. But at last, she admitted, "I'm still in a lot of pain."

"Do you know what is causing it?" Pablo looked worried.

"The doctors in the U.S. did not know what the problem was. They wanted to do a biopsy, but I was afraid and said no."

"Why? You need to do what they suggest."

"I didn't want them to put me to sleep."

"Do they even do that?"

"I don't know, but I didn't want it. Maybe my doctor here will have the answer."

"Let's hope so."

She went to see her doctor early the next morning. After a little small talk about how long it had been, she explained her situation—the pain inher backside she experienced daily, the difficulties using the bathroom, and how it could be hard to sit. He examined the area carefully, andafter a moment, he spoke up. "I can see that you have some growths down there. The condition you have is painful, but we can treat it. There's a medication we have used for the last 40 years that has been very effective. We can try it right now, and hopefully, you will feel better almost immediately."

Noemi breathed a sigh of relief. "That is what I've been waiting to hear. Let's do it today."

He explained the procedure, saying, "When I apply this medicine, it will hurt because it is killing the growths. That is normal."

Noemi thought she was ready, but as the treatment began, she jumped and yelled. "It hurts like hell!" she cried.

"It will only be another minute," he said soothingly.

Noemi continued to yell at the top of her lungs. Then, at last, it was over. When her doctor told her to come back in a week for one more treatment, she gasped, "What? I have to go through that again?"

"Yes, but now you will know what to expect, so it will be easier."

Noemi left his office, barely able to walk for the pain and hobbled the few blocks to Pablo's apartment. Though she continued to feel uncomfortable for the next two days, she concentrated on enjoying her granddaughters, her son, and her friends. She also talked with Tomevery day. She was, however, less than honest when he asked how her doctor visit went, only saying, "It was fine. I have to go back for anothervisit, but just a check-up. I'm really glad that I got to see my doctor.

She did not explain the seriousness of her pain because she didn't want him to worry.

Her next visit was even worse than the first. To begin with, the pain of the medication was just as bad. She jumped and screamed as he applied the treatment. Then, after, he told her, "I need to see you again next week."

"I won't be here next week. I leave for Ecuador tomorrow."

The doctor looked at her with a serious expression. "Noemi, this problem is more severe than most, and I think you will need to continue the treatments."

"You're kidding me. Do I need more of this? I don't think I can even walk home today."

"Here, I will write down some instructions, and you can give this to your Ecuadoran doctor so they can continue with this."

"How many more treatments do you think I will need?"

"I don't know Noemi, as many as it takes. We have to kill all of these growths before you are better. You do want to be better, don't you?"

"Of course."

"Then, you need to continue these treatments."

Noemi was not happy with the discussion, but she knew that the doctor was right. After six years of pain, she was tired of it and just wanted it to go away. When Pablo took her to the airport the next morning, she admitted, "This pain that I told you about the past few years will not stop. I've been to several doctors, and none of them seem to know what is wrong or how to treat it. I don't know what to do."

"There must be something they can do to help treat the pain while they look for a remedy. You should never have to suffer so much."

"I'm going to continue this treatment in Ecuador. Maybe eventually it will cure me of whatever I have."

Salinas, Ecuador

On the way back to their condo, Noemi explained to Tom what the doctor said, how he had diagnosed her problem, and what he recommended to help her.

"I have never heard of that condition," Tom said, "Will these treatments kill them?"

Noemi replied, "My doctor thinks so. We will see. But let's not talk about it anymore. Let me tell you about the conversation I had with another Vietnam vet on the plane."

Noemi explained what the man had said on the flight to Argentina, and how Tom might qualify for disability due to PTSD.

Tom wasn't having any of it. "That guy is nuts. I don't have PTSD, and I am not disabled. I wasn't even wounded over there."

Noemi decided to drop the subject, at least for now.

The next day, Noemi went looking for a doctor to continue her treatments in Ecuador, and soon discovered that Guayaquil was the best place. Soon she found herself in the exam room of a proctology specialist there while Tom waited in the reception area. She explained her problem and gave the doctor the treatment instructions her Argentine physician had written up.

"We don't have that here," the doctor explained, "But let me examine the area." She looked for a moment then confirmed, "Yes, I agree with your doctor's diagnosis. The treatment which we recommend is nitrogen."

"What the heck is that?"

"Nitrogen freezes the growths and kills them. You have twenty or more, so it will take several treatments to kill them all."

"Will this treatment hurt?"

"Yes, you will have some discomfort. I can start today, and we will do another each week for a month or so."

"Wow, that long?"

"Maybe longer, depending on how your body reacts to the nitrogen."

"How long will each treatment last?"

"About ten minutes."

Noemi took a deep breath. "Okay, let's get started."

The pain was not nearly as sharp as the Argentine method, but it still hurt. At least it was quick, Noemi thought. She told Tom this on the way back to Salinas and explained that she would need to come back several times.

"Well, I hope these treatments do the job. You need to get well."

"No shit," Noemi grumbled.

Unfortunately, after several weeks, she felt no better, and the symptoms were the same as always, she said to Tom. "These treatments aren't working. The pain will not go away. I don't know what to do. I am so tired of hurting. I have to find a solution."

"Then call and cancel your next appointment. We'll try something else."

Next, Noemi decided she was tired of traditional doctors who were not helping her. Maybe something homeopathic would be the solution. She found someone in Cuenca, and they made the five-hour trip to see him. The homeopathic doctor recommended a salve and a daily IV of vitamin C. They would do this for five days, then cut back to once a month.

Noemi's treatment lasted an hour each day, and they explored the city of Cuenca with their free time. Like New Mexico, the city was at a high altitude and had cool weather. They bought jackets, took a bus tour around the city, and went shopping at the mall.

Noemi had high hopes for the new homeopathic methods. She returned to Chipipe uncertain whether her body felt better yet, but confident that this was the answer she had been searching for. The couple went back to Cuenca twice more for her monthly treatments; then, it was time for their annual trip to New Mexico. Before they left, Noemi finally admitted to Tom, "I'm not getting better. The pain is getting worse. I am going to a doctor for a biopsy. I have got to see what is going on with my body."

"I agree."

Taos County, NM

Once they were back at the cabin, Tom and Noemi went straight to an urgent care facility. They had no primary care physician, and unlike Latin America, they couldn't simply go to a specialist on their own. So, they had to pay a visit to the "doc in the box" first. When this physician examined her, he made an appointment for a biopsy right away.

Noemi was nervous about the procedure since she did not want anyone cutting on her, but the little surgery turned out not to be so bad. The hard part was two days later when the phone rang, and Tom answered to find the surgeon's office on the other end. They wanted Noemi to come in for the doctor to read the results. "Why can't you just read it to us over the phone?" they wanted to know.

"It does not work that way," the receptionist explained. "The doctor wants to see Noemi and talk to her." They made the appointment, but they felt as though they already knew what the results would be.

It was an anxious few days before the next appointment. Then, they found themselves sitting in front of the doctor, who started by saying, "There is no easy way to say this, so I will tell you that you have stage two anal cancer. There is no place in Taos for treatment, but I can set you up with an appointment in Santa Fe."

Tom was extremely surprised that Noemi did not break down. Instead, she seemed to find strength in knowing at last what the problem was, after nine long years of pain. All the different doctors, all the different treatments…all of it had been for nothing.

Tom was proud that she brought the same determination to this as she did everything else. Once they got back to the cabin, Noemi got on the computer and began her research. Day and night, she read about every single treatment for cancer in the entire world. She chatted with cancer survivors on the Internet, and with others local in Taos. She interviewed anyone and everyone willing to talk to her about the treatment, and then she researched those treatments.

Tom and Noemi spent most of their days discussing the many options. Together, they went to cancer group therapy sessions in Taos. Therethey found patients who shared their experiences, successes, and failures. Most of these individuals went through chemotherapy, so Noemi researched chemotherapy and quickly learned that it killed more patients than it cured. She decided right away that that treatment was notfor her. She found a local nutritionist and began to buy natural remedies,changed her diet, and only bought organic foods. Tom blended all sorts of concoctions for her. They even bought a juicer for exotic recipes that included blueberries, turmeric, garlic, carrots, beets, and who knows what else.

While all of this was good for Noemi, and it helped to strengthen both her immune system and her emotional wellbeing, none of it helped the constant pain. Someone recommended THC, so the couple drove to Colorado, where marijuana was legal and bought THC capsules for her to take as an enema. They drove another three hundred miles to adifferent Colorado city where they could buy a food grade 35% peroxide solution that she could use to soak in the bathtub.

At last, she had to admit that nothing so far had worked. A doctor recommended the last hope, a treatment called hyperthermia, which involved the targeted use of heat, and you can only find that in California. Noemi discovered that the treatment center would see her, but Medicare would only cover it if she agreed to radiation as part of the therapy regimen.

This was the opposite of what she wanted, but Noemi was tired. More than anything else, she wanted to feel good again. She agreed to the combination of hyperthermia and radiation. Because the clinic was the only one of its kind in the U.S., and a very busy place, appointment was scheduled several months out. All they could do was wait.

15
We Were Soldiers

Taos, NM

One evening, Tom and Noemi decided to blow off a little steam with a night at the casino. They drove into Taos. When they arrived, Tom dropped Noemi at the front door and went to park the car. He put on his Vietnam Veteran ball cap, walked across the lot, and making his way to the door. A man walking out of the building stopped, looked at Tom's hat, and said, "What percent are you?"

Tom stared back, baffled, "I don't know what you mean."

"Disability, what percent are you?"

"I am not disabled!"

The guy snorted, "Oh, yes, you are. If you were in Vietnam, you are disabled. I have PTSD. I am 100% disabled… and so are you."

Tom just stared, so the man went on, "The local VA rep is named Michael. You need to call him and make an appointment."

"Sure, I will."

"I'm serious; you need to call him." When the guy said goodbye, Tom went inside to find Noemi. He told her what had happened. They agreed that when they got home, Tom should make that call. And he did.

Tom made the appointment, but he still wasn't convinced. "This is a waste of time. I do not have PTSD, and I am not disabled."

"It will not hurt to find out."

"I'm going," he promised. And he was true to his word. Parking was terrible when he arrived in Taos that morning, so he rushed into his appointment with only seconds to spare. In a tiny room, he found one little older man behind a desk. This was Michael. Tom explained, "I met a veteran on the street yesterday, and he told me that I needed to come to see you."

"I see," Michael replied, moving to the computer at a small, cluttered desk. "What branch of the service were you in?"

"Marine Corps!"

"Did you participate in any war?"

"Vietnam."

"What was your job there?"

"I was a machine gunner."

"Wow, boots on the ground. What years?"

"1968 and 1969."

"Were you honorably discharged?"

"Yes."

If Tom thought this was the whole process, he was wrong. It was just the beginning. Michael explained that he had just been put "in thesystem" and would need to see a psychiatrist at the VA clinic next. Thenhe would come back to Michael. Tom left, wondering about this strange little man, and what he'd just gotten himself into. But he called the VA clinic, in Taos, as instructed and was told he would have to see a social worker before he could even get an appointment with the psychiatrist.

Well, this just kept getting better. Tom made the appointment anyway, and when he hung up the phone, he turned to Noemi, "Dang, things are moving quickly. I have an appointment in the morning."

"Great!"

Tom had no idea what to expect from the social worker when he arrived at the VA clinic the next morning. When he walked in, he could see six other older men waiting, along with three girls working away behind a glass wall. He waited nervously until a door swung open, and a woman called out, "Mr. Bradburn?" He stood and followed her down a hallway to a tiny office.

At first, she sat at a computer, and Tom sat behind her. She asked about his service, and he realized she was reading all the information that Michael had submitted. Then she swiveled her chair around to face him and asked, "Can you tell me about your experiences in Vietnam?"

"What do you want to know?"

"I want to know if you ever saw any action over there, and if so, tell me what you saw and how you felt."

Tom got quiet as he stared at the wall to his left for a moment and thought, "I have never shared these thoughts or feelings with anyone before." The social worker sat forward into her chair and looked in his face, and Tom started to talk. "I was involved in many firefights. I was a machine gunner."

"Did you ever see anyone get hurt?"

He took a long moment before answering. His eyes began to water. "Yes. I saw many of my friends get hurt."

"Do you ever have nightmares about those experiences?"

"Yes, I have three recurring nightmares."

"Can you share them with me?"

He did not want to talk about this, but he carried on. "We were in a firefight one evening, and a close friend of mine was next to me. It was one of our first firefights, and we were both scared shitless as the bullets were flying past us. Then he was shot in the head, and I saw him fall, and he died instantly. I turned him over and saw the blood pouring from his forehead." Tears began to run down his cheeks, and he fell silent.

She let him sit for a moment, then asked, "Are you okay, Mr. Bradburn?"

Tom took a breath, "Yep. I'm okay. On another occasion, we were in a terrible firefight, and one of our beloved gunnies, who was about ten yards in front of me, tripped a wire, and an explosive went off. It blew one of his legs off, and the other was bleeding terribly. I ran to his side, and I fell on top of him to protect him from the bullets while we waited for the medic. He was in so much pain he was screaming in my ear. I kept telling him that he would be okay, but he continued to yell. Then the medic appeared and pulled me away from the gunny, and the medic took over. I never saw him again. I heard that he lost both legs and was evacuated to a hospital and then finally home to his family."

He looked away again until she leaned forward once more. Coming back to reality, Tom continued, "The third nightmare, I don't understand why I have it. One day, I was in the rear area, and mortars began coming in. The siren began to ring, and everyone headed outside to the trenches. I jumped in a trench, and my buddy, the company mail clerk, jumped in beside me. The mortars were nonstop for a few minutes, and everyone had their heads tucked between their legs. Once the mortars let up, my friend looked up from the trench, and another one exploded close by. He took a piece of shrapnel to his cheek. Once we all stood up, I saw the blood running down his face. It was nothing major, but it hit him. I called out for the medic, who came quickly. All was okay, and my buddy only received a couple of stitches. I don't understand why I have nightmares about that incident, but I do."

The social worker handed Tom a tissue, and he wiped his eyes. She was frantically pecking at her keyboard. "What are you typing?"

"I'm entering all of this information into your record book." She turned around to face him again. "Tell me about your anxiety attacks."

Once again, Tom had to sit for what felt like forever before he could speak. "Sometimes, out of nowhere, I get very shaky and nervous. I begin to sweat, and I feel like I'm going to jump out of my skin. There are times when I feel as though I will pass out. My heart begins pounding. I have to sit for a while to regain my senses. Those are the most terrifying moments I have ever experienced."

"How often do you experience these attacks?"

"It's hard to say. It varies, but at least once a month."

"How long have you had these attacks?" "Fifty

years. Since Vietnam."

"Well, Mr. Bradburn," She said, "You certainly have PTSD. Would you like me to make you an appointment to see the physiatrist?"

Tom said, "I suppose so. What will he do for me?"

"He will prescribe medication for you."

"I'm not sure that I need medication, but okay," he agreed to an appointment with the doctor, and another appointment with the social worker in a few days, and started the drive home. On the way, thoughts of Vietnam filled his mind. It had been very difficult for him to discuss these things.

Taos County, NM

He was so quiet when he got home, that Noemi began to worry. She asked over and over, "Baby, are you okay?"

Tom would quickly reply, "Yes, I'm fine."

At last, she burst out, "No. You are not fine. Something is wrong. What is it?"

Tom tried to explain that it had been painful to talk about his experiences. She burst out, "That's it; I don't want you to see her again.I don't like this. You are different. I think you should call the VA and cancel that appointment."

Tom shook his head. "Nope, I need to go."

VA Clinic, Taos, NM

The next appointment was uncomfortable in an entirely new way. When the young woman led him down the long hallway and into an office, only a computer sat at the desk. She explained, "This will be a teleconference. Just have a seat, and once the doctor is ready, he will appear on the screen. Then the two of you can have a conversation."

It was eerily quiet, as Tom waited in front of the screen, then without warning, a person popped up on the screen. It was a man Tom's age, and he said, "Good morning, my name is Doctor Geese. How are you?"

Tom looked at the face on the screen. "I have never had a doctor's appointment like this. I don't suppose I will be getting any injections today, huh?"

The man laughed, "No, I'm not that kind of doctor." He looked at Tom's record, reviewed the history of anxiety attacks, nightmares, and anger issues, and explained, "I'm going to prescribe some medication for you to help with each of these conditions."

Tom frowned. "I don't like medication. I've never taken anything in my life except for aspirin."

"Let's start with low doses and see how they work. You'll get them in the mail within three days." He asked Tom to make a follow-up appointment for two weeks, and then as quickly as he had appeared, he disappeared from the screen. Tom was amazed at how short and simple it had been.

The next stop, a few days later, was another visit to Michael. The strange little man reviewed Tom's appointments and asked about the prescriptions. He confirmed that he had more appointments. Then he had Tom fill out a paper with many questions, including the name of his unit and any prior medical attention he may have received from the military. Of course, Tom entered his anxiety attack at El Toro and his useless encounters with the physiatrist at the VA in Dallas. Michael printed copies of this form and faxed them someplace, and then instructed him, "Tom, continue your appointments and build your record and you will receive a notice in the mail in a month or so."

"When do I see you again?"

"You probably will not see me again."

"What? Why won't I see you again?"

Michael said, "I'm done with my work. Now, it's all up to you."

On the drive home, Tom thought a lot about those last words.

Taos County, NM

For the next weeks, he did as Michael had instructed. He kept his appointments and took his meds. After the first few days, Noemi announced, "Baby, you are a different man."

"What do you mean, different?"

"You are more relaxed and happier. I love it!"

Tom didn't quite know what to make of this, but it sounded like he should keep doing it, whatever it was. At first, Noemi worried about his return to the social worker, because she remembered how troubled he had been after his last visit. But Tom felt different as he sat in the woman's office. He felt more relaxed, even witty, and jovial. The social worker noticed the difference right away. She commented, "I notice here that you received your medication from doctor Geese, and I can tell that you have been taking it."

He smiled, "You know, Noemi told me the same thing. I cannot tell the difference, but Noemi said that I seem to be a different man."

"It's true. I noticed right away, too. Welcome back to reality," shesmiled. And there was no more talk of Vietnam or war or blood andguts. Instead, they discussed Tom's everyday life and how that was going. When this session finished, he was glad to schedule another appointment.

When he got home, Noemi said, "Baby, you are like a new man. You are the Tom, I remember."

Albuquerque, NM

Two weeks before Noemi was scheduled to begin treatment at the California clinic, Tom had received a notice from the VA that he needed to see the resident psychologist at the Albuquerque VA Hospital. And now he was sitting in a small room in the huge hospital.

A large woman walked in, her whole body radiating a no-nonsense, matter-of-fact attitude. She explained, "This meeting will take approximately three hours. I will ask you a series of true or false questions and then a series of multiple-choice questions. We will go back in forth in that manner until we are finished. Do you understand?"

"Yes."

Then the questions started, rapid-fire. Tom felt ambushed. He thought that several of them had multiple possible answers and wanted to think before he answered. She appeared irritated. "I need you to answer these questions quickly. Do not think about it. I need the first answer that comes to your mind."

"But some of these questions have two different answers, and I want to give you the right one."

She raised her voice, "The first answer that comes to your mind."

Now Tom was feeling annoyed himself. "Okay, okay!"

She dove right back in:

"Have you ever considered suicide?"

"Have you ever killed anyone?"

"Do you enjoy killing people?"

On and on and on, this continued for three solid hours. At last, the psychologist said, "Okay, Mr. Bradburn, this will be the last question. Are you ready?

"Yep, I'm ready."

"Okay, here goes. Has it crossed your mind to kill me today?"

Tom chuckled, "You know it has."

She did not smile back. "Yes or no, Mr. Bradburn."

Tom snipped, "Yes."

Then, it was over. On the three-hour trip home, Tom wondered about the purpose of the format. Did she want to confuse or upset him? Trick him into saying the wrong things? He was glad it was over. And he knew he could never properly explain what had happened to Noemi because he was not certain himself.

In any case, Noemi's treatments would begin very soon. He knew where all of his focus would need to be during that time. Tom suspended all of his VA appointments for the foreseeable future, explaining that he would be in California for at least six weeks.

16
California Promises

Taos County, NM

As they prepared for their drive to California, Noemi considered the changes in Tom's behavior. He was so much better, now that he was receiving the help that he had always needed. One day, she went to him and said, "Baby, I would never have said this a month ago. But you are doing so well now, how would you feel about getting married again?"

Tom was delighted. "You know what? I've been thinking the same thing. I do love you, and I don't know what I'd do if I did not have you in my life."

They both felt like children, planning their trip to the courthouse. Before they knew it, they were standing in front of a judge as she said, "I now pronounce you man and wife. "Over dinner that night, Tom observed, "It never seemed like we were divorced. I love you, and I'm happy that you wanted me back."

The only thing that disrupted their happiness was the looming start of Noemi's treatment. She called the clinic each day to check-in, and they explained that they'd schedule her for a total of thirty-three treatments, five per week for a total of seven weeks. She was shocked to discover it would take so long, but when she told Tom, he shrugged, "It is what it is."

With her continued pain and discomfort, she also worried about the long car trip. All of that sitting seemed impossible. But if they were going to be in California for an extended stay, they needed their car. She packed for the trip as though they were going to remodel a house in Roswell. They were planning for every scenario, except for the mattress, ofcourse.

One bright spot was learning that the American Cancer Society would help with their housing. They made a booking to stay at a motel during their trip, with the assurance that ACS would pay the cost.

At last, the day came for their departure, and Noemi was a bundle of nerves. But she was also full of hope and excitement that pain-free days might await her in the future. Thanks to his new meds and counseling support, Tom was still his happy self and made many jokes along the way. This gave Noemi strength, and they tackled the drive like teenagers, only stopping when Noemi became uncomfortable, needed topee, needed to eat, or they needed fuel.

California State, USA

The couple had no problems with maps or navigation…until they hit the California border. That is when the maps became less accurate. This was the days before everyone had GPS in their car, and they drove around, lost for what seemed like forever. In the early morning hours, tired and frustrated, Noemi called the motel where they had reservations. The man who answered was half asleep and gave terrible directions. Now they were more lost than before.

They were ready to give up, but they came upon an open convenience store. Tom went inside, and thankfully, the clerk knew exactly where the Santa Monica Extended Stay America was. He gave great directions and soon they were there. Once again, they woke up the night clerk, and he grumpily checked them in. When they got to their room, however, they found the bathtub full of dirty towels. Once more, they woke the clerk, and he found them a different room.

Exhausted, they decided to deal with unloading the car in the morning. At 3:30 am, after 17 hours in the car, they collapsed on the bed and quickly fell asleep. They slept very late the next morning, which was, luckily, a free day. Over breakfast, they decided to drive around and locate the hyperthermia clinic, so that it would be easier to find on treatment days.

The clinic was approximately thirty minutes from the motel and not easy to find. The couple had to get on and off of several freeways to get there. It took another half an hour to find a parking place. The building itself was huge, and they had to read through a long list of doctors' names on a board to discover that their clinic was on the 10th floor. Theymade the long elevator ride, then wandered down a long hallway, checking the numbers on each door they passed. At last, there it was.

They entered to find an empty waiting room. There were no patients or staff in sight. They had to make a thorough search of the entire room before they found the receptionist at last, at a desk tucked away behind a wall. The young woman, Lynn, immediately recognized Noemi's voice. After all, they had spoken on the phone every week for the last three months. They greeted each other with a big hug before Lynn asked, "What brings you here today? Your appointment is for tomorrow."

"We just wanted to find the building and your office today so that we don't have to waste time tomorrow searching for you."

Lynn smiled, "Wow, I wish all of our patients thought like you."

They said goodbye to Lynn, promising to be on time the next day, and headed back to the motel. When she stopped by the office to request towels, the clerk called Noemi over. "You're aware that The American Cancer Society only has you scheduled at this motel for one week, aren't you?"

"What? Will we be here for seven weeks or longer? I told them so. How can this be?"

"I don't know, but they do this all the time. That's why I thought I should say something to you now."

Noemi stormed back to their room, and flung open the door, shouting, "Do you know what they did?"

Tom looked up, startled. "What who did?"

"That American Cancer Society."

"What did they do?"

"We can only stay here for a week, and then we have to move."

"What are we going to do?"

Noemi shook her head. "I don't know. I'll talk to Lynn tomorrow and see what she says."

Fortunately, Noemi's anger had subsided the next morning. As she dressed for her first appointment, she called out to Tom, "You know what?"

In a playful tone, he replied, "No, I was hoping you would tell me what."

"I love you."

He walked over and kissed her. "And I love you too, little girl."

Noemi and Tom were glad they had taken the time to find the office. Today they didn't have to search for Lynn's reception desk. After a short wait, they were taken back to a conference room and introduced to Dr. Streeter and his assistant CJ. They asked about the drive from New Mexico and made small talk for a few moments, to put Noemi at ease. Then Dr. Streeter explained that he would do a preliminary examination and show the couple a short film on the procedure.

Dr. Streeter was a big, burly African American, with a smile that lit the room. Noemi liked him right away. He was careful and gentle during the exam and explained every step to Noemi, CJ, and the nurse as if he were teaching a class. She was very relieved that he had not been as rough as some of her other doctors, and that he had treated her with kindness.

Shortly after the exam, they all sat together in front of a projector. The nurse turned out the lights, and the film began. Doctor Streeter described what everyone was viewing, which was how the hyperthermia machine works and the technology behind it. When it ended, he asked, "Okay, do you understand the equipment that we will be using?"

"Yes, it's fascinating!" Noemi replied.

"Well, if you do understand, you're smarter than all of us." Dr. Streeter and his staff laughed. "CJ, will you go over the steps for tomorrow's procedure?"

CJ stood. "Noemi, do you remember the table and the hyperthermia machine in the movie?"

"Yes."

"Well, in the morning, you will lie on that table on your side facing away from the wall." He pointed toward the nurse. "And Nurse Jones will position you and the machine at the precise angles, and then the machine will be turned on. The machine works with water, as the video explained. Once the water has all evaporated, that's the conclusion ofthe treatment. Each treatment will last approximately forty-five minutes."

"That's all?"

"Yes, ma'am. Only forty-five minutes."

Noemi asked, "Will there be any pain"?

"None. No pain during the procedure. We will make you as comfortable as possible. We want this to be a pleasant but successful treatment."

Next, Dr. Streeter explained that he had scheduled her radiation therapy with Dr. Baron, whom he considered the best in the city. They were supposed to check in at his office at UCLA that afternoon.

Noemi's face shone with relief as they left the conference room. On their way out of the office, they stopped to explain the motel situation to Lynn. The receptionist frowned when she heard the news, and said, "Well, we do work with an independent group that buys houses, remodels them, and then hosts cancer patients during their treatments. The problem is, they stay full. I will contact them again to see if they have a vacancy."

"Please, we're getting desperate."

"I'll see what I can do."

As usual, the couple had some trouble finding first UCLA and then suitable parking. But they found Dr. Baron's office quickly, and no sooner than they checked in, a nurse called them into the examination room. The couple sat quietly and nervously as they waited. Then Dr. Baron appeared. Like Dr. Streeter, he began with an examination and by talking to Noemi about her symptoms. Then he explained how he would calculate the correct dosage and the specific location for the radiation in her treatment.

Ever mindful, Noemi asked, "Will there be pain?"

"No. But there will likely be some burning for some time after. And the area of treatment will become very sensitive. That's normal."

"Oh my."

Now he smiled gently. "Don't worry, we are going to take extremely good care of you, and you will heal quickly. Based on what I have seen, I believe I can guarantee you 100% positive results with this treatment."

"How soon can we get started?"

"Tomorrow morning, after your hyperthermia treatment."

With that, the consultation was over, and Tom and Noemi made their way to their car. Noemi exhaled nervously, "Wow, very quick. Everything is so very quick."

Tom replied, "Thank the Lord for that."

On the way home, Tom spotted an In-N-Out Burger. As a restaurant professional, he had heard about them for years. They were legendary. "I have to have one of those!" He burst out.

Noemi giggled, "Let's go."

Like everywhere else in L.A., the crowd was terrible, and the drive-thru had twenty cars waiting in line. They parked and went inside to find each line was five or six people deep. People loved In-N-Out. And when he finished his burger, he could see why. It was one of the best burgers he had ever had.

Noemi slept badly due to anxiety, but they started early for the clinic the next day. Parking was even worse than the day before, and Tom let Noemi out at the curb because the clock was ticking. He drove around and around but could find nothing. He had to expand his search to the blocks surrounding the clinic to find a space. It took forever. And thenhe had to make a four-block journey to the clinic itself.

At last, he made it. Noemi was waiting at the door. "Wow, I thought someone kidnapped you."

"No. I had to park in Chicago." They joined hands and walked inside.

In no time at all, Noemi was on the treatment table in Dr. Streeter's office. CJ helped her lie on her right side, and then put her in a very specific, slightly uncomfortable position. "You'll need to stay just like this for the whole treatment," he cautioned her. It was forty-five minuteslong.

After it was over, she told him, "You were right; there was no pain, but very tiring to hold that position for almost an hour."

"It will get easier with time. You did just fine. Now you only have thirty-two more, and you will be cancer-free."

Now they had to hustle out and get on the road. Their appointment with Dr. Barron was in 45 minutes, and the UCLA hospital was 15 miles away. That does not sound like a long distance to most people, but now

Tom and Noemi knew the traffic in California could be a game-changer, and that they had to hurry.

On the drive over, Noemi squeezed Tom's hand. "Baby, I am nervous. I did not want radiation, and now here I am having radiation."

"Don't worry, Doctors Streeter and Baron know what's best for you."

"I know, but I'm still nervous."

She was jittery the whole time they sat in Dr. Baron's waiting room. She fidgeted so badly that at last, Tom put a hand on her knee and said, "Whoa, Nelly." Then they called her back, and Noemi disappeared from his sight.

As he waited, Tom watched other patients come and go. He wondered what stage of treatment each of them was at. Some seemed to be in a terrible state, but most seemed happy and healthy. He wondered fretfully if Noemi's treatment was going well. Then, surprisingly quickly, she reappeared.

They walked together down the hallway, past the reception desk, down the stairway, and into the parking area. Noemi said, "The treatment was very easy, and the nurses were very gentle. The only problem was the cold table that I had to lay on."

Tom smiled with relief. "If the only problem was the cold table, you did not have a problem."

"I am so glad we found this place. Now I know everything will be okay. The Lord led us here, and all will be okay."

Tom said, "It makes me feel much better to hear you say that."

The only bad news of the day was from Lynn, who had not been able to find new housing for the couple. She promised to keep trying. This was unfortunate because their reservation at the Extended Stay was only for another two days.

After stopping for another IN-N-Out burger, they returned to the motel, where Noemi started a new campaign of research, this time for a place to stay. She stumbled on a site called "Airbnb." In the listings, she came upon a place that seemed nearby in Santa Monica. The pictures showed what appeared to be a mansion. At $500 per week, it was much cheaper than a hotel. She immediately made an appointment to look at thehouse.

It was a twenty-five-mile drive down highway 405 through awful traffic, but at last, they found themselves in front of the most beautiful house they had ever seen. A scraggly looking older man named Juanmet them at the door. He gave them a tour, which included the beautiful bedroom where they would sleep, then the kitchen, and the swimming pool. Noemi was amazed, "This is five hundred dollars a week?"

"Yes."

After a glance at Tom, she affirmed, "Okay. We will take it. We will not move until tomorrow, and we will stay here ten days at a time because we are awaiting another housing opportunity where we can stay for free,but I like it here."

Juan said, "I will need to know a few days in advance, so I will have time to rent this to someone else if necessary."

"No problem."

The next day, after her treatments, they moved all of their belongings to Juan's home. "Now I feel like a millionaire," Noemi beamed.

The house was farther from both Dr. Streeter and Dr. Baron's offices, and they had to get up much earlier in the morning, but Noemi was very happy staying there. They spent their afternoons sitting by the pool. The bed in their room was high off the floor, just like the bed in their cabin, and they slept well. And in the morning, Tom was able to make hot tea for his queen. He boiled water in a pan with sliced ginger, put lime and honey in a cup, and dropped in a teabag, feeling happy that he could do this. It would not have been possible in a hotel. He brought it up to their room, and it was waiting when she opened her eyes. Her smile was the best reward he could have asked for. Then he went downstairs to make her breakfast.

Once breakfast was eaten and the dishes cleaned, the couple began their trip to Noemi's treatments. The traffic was the worst Tom had seen. As they crawled down highway 405 toward Santa Monica Blvd. he said, "No wonder there are more fatal accidents in New Mexico than in California. Here, a person cannot drive fast enough to hurt anyone." Noemi laughed.

Once again, Tom dropped Noemi at the door of the clinic, then circled for what seemed like hours looking for a parking spot. By the time hegot upstairs, she was already in the treatment room. He greeted Lynnand asked, "Were you able to find us a place to stay?"

"Not yet, but I heard that you guys are staying in a mansion."

Tom rolled his eyes. "Yes, and it costs a mansion price as well."

Lynn laughed. "Maybe I'll get lucky and find you a new place in a day or two."

Two weeks of treatments passed. They spent their free time on Santa Monica beach, or wandering around Whole Foods, or investigating different areas such as Hollywood and Beverly Hills. Then on the twelfth day, they walked into Dr. Streeter's office, and Lynn greeted them by saying, "I found you a place to stay!" There was an opening at one of the remodeled homes, and they could move in right away. "Now the bad news," she said seriously.

Noemi looked up, holding her breath. "Uh-oh. What has happened?"

"Now, you will have to move out of the millionaire house," she smiled. The three laughed together before CJ arrived to escort Noemi into the treatment area.

Though they had enjoyed their afternoons sunning by the pool, they were both glad to move. The new place was just off Santa Monica

Blvd., meaning they were close to both doctor's offices. They were sharing the home with three other families, each of which had a bedroom and private bathroom, together with a shared kitchen and laundry room. That meant Tom could continue making breakfast and tea for Noemi in the little house. Their housemates were all polite, but every family seemed to keep to itself.

Tom found that he enjoyed the tree-lined walking and bicycle path close by. After breakfast each day, he would take a stroll. He met a couple of retired military guys and started walking with them. Though neither was a combat veteran, he still found lots to talk about with them. Many times, they would break out in loud laughter as they walked and talked, and soon Tom was up to four miles a day of exercise.

They had another reason to be glad for the change. Their cash had been steadily dwindling due to the cost of the Airbnb rental, meals out, and $4.00 per gallon gasoline. Both checking accounts were seriously depleted, which caused them both stress and worry. On the third day in the new house, however, Tom returned from his morning walk to find Noemi was dancing and singing in the bedroom. "What the heck is going on?" He asked.

"Baby! Baby! You won't believe," she was clapping her hands.

Tom grinned. "Ok. What won't I believe?"

Noemi shouted out, "I checked your bank account, and the VA paid you. I had to look four or five times before I could believe it. You have to look right now."

Tom went straight to the computer and opened his bank's website. There it was. Tom nearly fell out of his chair. "There must be some mistake," he gasped.

"It's not a mistake," Noemi insisted, "You deserve that after what you went through for your country."

Tom looked again, then refreshed the page and looked again. The money was still there. He navigated to the VA disability rate page, comparing data for compensation. He figured out that his payment was based on being married with no children, at a 70% disability rating. "The VA says that I am 70% disabled," he marveled. Tom could not believe his eyes. "The Lord is so great. Every time we are in need, he is there."

Noemi replied, "When I saw that, I screamed. I'm surprised that you could not hear me on your walk. It is simply incredible!"

A few days later, Tom got his first standard monthly VA payment. Suddenly, it seemed that the couple was floating in cash.

And more good news followed. Noemi's treatments were halfway complete, and she had begun to notice the pain receding. She was beginning to move around better too. It looked like the hyperthermia and radiation were working.

One day, they witnessed an event that made them see not everyone shared their good fortune. They came back from Whole Foods to find the house swarming with police. As soon as they walked in, officers began to question them: "Are you staying here?" "How long have you stayed here? What time did you leave here this morning?" And on and on and on.

Finally, Noemi stopped them. "What is going on here?"

A female officer said, "Wait for a moment. My superior will come to talk to you in a minute."

A lieutenant appeared and stood with them. "We have had an incident here, and it is not a pleasant one. One of the cancer patients in this house has died."

"Oh my gosh, I'll bet it was the older lady who was staying here with her son," Noemi burst out.

"Yes ma'am, the Robinson family, James and Sarah."

"Where is James? Is he okay?"

"He's sitting on the back steps."

Tom and Noemi rushed out to find James with his elbows on his knees and his hands covering his eyes. They went immediately to embrace him. James began to cry out loud. In a broken voice, he said, "I left for a few minutes, and when I returned, she was lying on the floor, and she was gone. I was only away for a few minutes!"

They gave him a moment to calm down before Tom asked, "What will you do now?"

"I don't know. After all these treatments, the pain and problems that she dealt with…" He shook his head, "All of that was for nothing."

Tom patted his shoulder. "James, it was not for nothing. It allowed you to spend more time with Sarah than you otherwise would have. When she passed, you are the one who was closer to her than anyone else, and you are the only one she was thinking of."

James looked up and reached for Tom's hand. "Thanks, Tom. I needed to hear that." He took a breath. "My brother will come to me tonight. We'll load all of our things and leave very late. I'm glad I was able to meet the two of you."

Tom said, "James, you are a very strong man, and we are grateful to have met you and Sarah."

The next days were difficult for Noemi. James had left in the night, and she thought a lot about Sarah. They had shared the common thread of a cancer diagnosis, and now Sarah was gone. Noemi didn't want to stay in the house any longer. It was too painful. But Tom reminded her, "We only have eight more days left. One week and one day. It would be impossible for us to find a better situation with such short notice. Let's tough it out." Noemi agreed this was for the best.

In addition to the shock and grief, she was also in increasing physical discomfort. As predicted, she began to feel burning sensations from the radiation. The nurses had assured her that it was normal and would start to disappear a couple of weeks after the treatment ended. But after putting up with pain for so many years, Noemi was not sure how she would stand it.

On her last day of treatment, Dr. Streeter's clinic held a little celebration for Noemi. Someone in the office folded a piece of paper into a beautiful swan and gave it to her, and all twelve doctors, nurses, and staff came to hug Noemi and to wish her well. Then, when their car pulled into the parking lot for the last visit to UCLA, Noemi looked at Tom and said, "Baby. I have so much burning pain that I want to skip this last treatment. I do not think I can do this."

He looked at her thoughtfully. "You should at least go inside and tell the nurses what you are thinking."

"You are right; they at least deserve that. Wait here for a minute, and I will be right back."

Noemi went upstairs and shared her feelings with the staff. The nurses responded sternly that Dr. Baron had planned her treatment carefully, and that all thirty-three sessions were necessary for it to be successful. They promised that she could have a prescription for a cream to help with the pain, but insisted that she have the last radiation session.

At last, Noemi returned to the car. "What happened," Tom asked, "You were in there for a long time."

"Well, the girls talked me into having the final treatment. They also gave me a little send-off like Dr. Streeter's people did. It was such a great feeling for them to do that for me. I'm sorry you missed it."

Tom nodded. "I'm glad. Now we will always know that you did your part."

"Give me a kiss," replied Noemi. Tom obliged, and then they drove away from UCLA for the last time.

17
Forever and Ever Amen

Taos County, NM

The drive home was long, but at least they did not need maps. They walked into the cabin with great relief and put their things away. Then Tom took Noemi in a tight hug, "I'm very proud of you."

She sighed, "Thank you, Baby. I am so happy to be home now."

The next step was to arrange visits with her local doctors. First up was her primary care physician. During the exam, the doctor expressed surprise and pleasure that there was no evidence of cancer. "You'll need an MRI to prove that you are cancer-free, but from what I can see, there is no sign of it like before."

Next came a visit to the oncologist, who also found no signs of cancer. "You look so much better!" she said and agreed that an MRI was the way to confirm the good news.

Noemi knew from her experience at UCLA that she did not like MRIs. The tube made her feel claustrophobic. But she did as her doctors asked and scheduled one for the next Monday.

Taos, NM

After two difficult months, Noemi wanted a chance to relax and unwind, so they headed once again for the casino in Taos. Like before, Tom dropped her off out front and went to the park. And once again, he met someone important at the door: Michael. Tom shook his hand and thanked him for his part in securing the 70% disability status. He also said, "You know I called you from California the same day I received my disability pay. I wanted to thank you, but I got no answer. Then I tried several more times and still no answer. I thought something was wrong."

Michael shook his head. "I retired!" he explained. "I'm glad to hear your news. But you, my friend, need to apply for unemployability."

"What the heck is that?"

"That is what will get you to 100% disability. Go to the VA office tomorrow and talk with the new representative and get that process started." They shook hands, and Tom went to find Noemi.

The very next day, Tom drove back to Taos to meet the new VA representative...only to find a note taped to the door. They had moved the office to the city of Raton, 100 miles away. On the way home, Tom decided to stop by the VA clinic and make his usual appointments. There he discovered that his social worker was no longer employed there, and they did not have a replacement for her yet. It seems that the VA signed a contract with a new company, and there was a shakeup at the Taos clinic. Many of the friendly faces that he had known were now gone. He did learn that the new representative would have office hoursin Taos the next day and made an appointment.

Noemi and Tom drove up together. In the car, he said, "I hope this guy is half as helpful as Michael was."

"Don't worry; he will be."

They met Robert Barnum, the new representative, in a small conference room. Tom explained that Michael had recommended applying for unemployability. Robert clarified that this would require Tom's last employer to fill out a form. He walked them through the process, and the couple realized this wasn't going to be as simple as they had hoped. On the way back to the car, Tom commented, "Wow, what a process. This will also take some time."

Noemi shrugged, "It is what it is." And they laughed. The next morning, Tom mailed the form to his last employer, and that was that. Now came the wait—for the form, and the results of Noemi's MRI.

To Tom's amazement, his old boss returned the form in approximately a week. He was able to call Robert and arrange a meeting in the town of Angel Fire. During the sixty-mile drive, the couple had plenty of time to enjoy the scenery and the beauty of the forest, as they did after their wedding.

They took a little time to visit the local Veteran's Memorial and wander through a museum that highlighted New Mexico veterans, and thenwent in to see Robert.

The man was surprised to see them so soon. "Many veterans have to wait months to receive these forms back, so congratulations to you!" he enthused. He looked over the materials and noted, "I see that in the past, you have had some real anger issues?"

"Yes," Tom admitted, "Yes, but thanks to the VA, I am past it."

"I can vouch for that," Noemi chimed in.

Robert set about faxing the form to another office, and as Tom watched, he asked, "Will I have any more meetings or appointments to make before we hear back about this?"

No. You will hear something within a month or so."

"Oh, good," Tom said, "We have a trip to Argentina planned."

Noemi spoke up again. "We're married, but we are not receiving the payment for a married veteran. What can we do to fix that?"

Now Robert looked at his records, confused. "Tom, your record shows you as single."

Tom and Noemi looked at each other, a bit embarrassed. Why go into the whole story? Tom said, "Nope, I'm married."

Robert typed at his computer for a moment, smiled up at them, and asked, "Anything else I can do for you?" The Bradburn's stood up,shook his hand, and thanked him for his time, then hit the road.

The next day also featured an important appointment: a visit to Noemi's oncologist to discuss the results of her MRI. The drive seemed to take forever. Then they spent ages in the doctor's waiting room. Then the nurse came and put Noemi through the endless process of weighing her, taking her to the exam room, and taking her temperature and blood pressure. At long last, the doctor opened the door, a glowing smile on her face. "Hello Noemi," she beamed, "You're looking great. And Ihave even greater news for you. Your MRI showed no—I repeat no— signs of cancer.

Noemi embraced her doctor. "That is the greatest news I have ever heard. Thank you. Thank you. Thank you for all that you have done for me," she said.

"My pleasure."

In the waiting room, Tom sat on the edge of his chair. The moment Noemi stepped through the door; he knew what the results were. He stood and took her in a tight hug. "How did you know," she laughed, "I haven't said a word!"

"I could see it on your face," he said. "Let's go home."

Buenos Aires, Argentina

Tom sat in the kitchen in the home of Noemi's friend, waiting for his wife to wake up. He drank coffee as he checked his email and Facebook, and then when he heard stirring in the bedroom, he took Noemi her tea.

When she was ready, they would walk the mile to a local restaurant for breakfast. For now, he would spend a little more time on his computer. His daily routine included checking his bank account at 11:30 Argentina

154

time, which signaled the start of the banking day in New Mexico time. Today, when he logged into his account, he met a shock.

The VA had deposited his disability, including back pay, into the account. Tom was now considered 100% disabled, total, and permanent.In a weak, crackly voice, he called, "Baby, could you come here for a minute?"

Worried that something was wrong, Noemi rushed to his side. He pointed at the screen. She looked at the numbers and shrieked in amazement. "Lord, Lord, Lord. You are so good to us. Why are you so good to us?" she cried.

"It's incredible," he replied. "After all those years, after all those tears, here it is." He had to admit, perhaps for the first time, that it was all true. He did have extreme anxiety. He did have a sleep disorder. He did have anger issues, and his back was permanently injured. Now, finally, he was being compensated for those years in the war, and their long after-effects. "You know, ever since Vietnam, I have known that something was not right with me. Thanks to your encouragement, and the VA, my life is on track, and I feel better than ever."

Tears in their eyes, the couple held each other tight. On this day, Noemi's health was as good as anyone on the planet. Tom's emotional problems were under control. And, at last, after so many years of gambling and hustling, their finances were guaranteed. They had a cabinhome in a beautiful mountain valley, an ocean view condo in Chipipe, Ecuador, and wonderful grandchildren in two different countries. Blessed by the hand of God, the future looked bright.

CPSIA information can be obtained
at www.ICGtesting.com
Printed in the USA
LVHW052140041121
702459LV00004B/111